MORTUARY LAW

Ninth Revised Edition

By

T. SCOTT GILLIGAN, J.D.

and

THOMAS F.H. STUEVE, A.B., L.L.B., A.M.

Published 1940
Revised 1946
Revised 1956
Reprinted 1960
Revised 1963
Revised 1966
Reprinted 1968
Reprinted 1971
Reprinted 1973
Revised 1975
Revised 1980
Reprinted 1982
Revised 1984
Revised 1988
Rewritten 1995

Published by The Cincinnati Foundation for Mortuary Education

645 W. North Bend Road

Cincinnati, Ohio 45224-1462

513/761-2020

ISBN 1-883031-01-X

To Shenandoah

PREFACE TO NINTH
REVISED EDITION

Tom Stueve's *Mortuary Law* has been the legal handbook of mortuary science students for over 50 years. On the occasion of its ninth revision, it has been my distinct privilege and honor to rewrite Tom's definitive tome on the subject of funeral law. It is my fervent hope that this ninth edition will live up to the high standards of scholarship that Tom Stueve has devoted to this important and fascinating subject for the past half century.

Tom Stueve often noted in prior revisions that the evolution of law is a slow but relentless process. However, in the past fifteen years the pace of change in mortuary law has been anything but slow. During that time, the funeral professional has encountered a dizzying array of federal regulations, novel theories of legal liability, and new responsibilities and obligations to employees, consumers and the families served by the profession. As a result, a rewrite of the entire book was required.

I would like to take this opportunity to thank Dan Flory, the President of the Cincinnati College of Mortuary Science for his assistance and patience, Thomas H. Clark, former General Counsel of the National Funeral Directors Association for his guidance, and Lynne Kunzelman and Vicky Beck for their invaluable secretarial assistance.

T. Scott Gilligan

Cincinnati, Ohio
January 2, 1995

TABLE OF CONTENTS

MORTUARY LAW

Chapter One

INTRODUCTION

1.1   Study of Mortuary Law

To be successful in funeral service, both as a caregiver and as a businessman, the funeral director must have a working knowledge of the many laws that impact the profession. This body of law, which is dynamic and growing, is defined for purposes of this book as "mortuary law" or "funeral law."

Funeral law consists of the rules and principles that society has established for the handling and disposition of the dead. It provides rights and places duties upon the survivors of the decedent so that the dead can be memorialized without jeopardizing the health and safety of the overall community. In so doing, that law also places upon funeral directors a detailed set of duties and obligations which they owe to the survivors of the decedent, the clients they contract with, their employees, and the community where the funeral home is located.

The purpose of this book is to give students sufficient knowledge of the substance and operation of funeral law so that they can fulfill their duties and obligations in a professional and ethical manner. The book will strive not to be simply a recital of statute and case laws, but more an explanation of what is required of the funeral director under the law.

1.2   Sources of Mortuary Law

Government regulation of business, especially the funeral profession, has greatly expanded in the past twenty years. The sources of that increasing regulatory scope are as follows:

a.   *State Laws and Regulations.*

The states are the principal regulators of the funeral profession. Each state has an inherent authority known as its police power. The police power empowers the state legislature to enact laws for the protection of the general welfare, health and safety. Included in this power is the authority to restrict individuals in the exercise of certain activities so as to promote the common good.

1

The police power of the state empowers it to set standards and requires licenses of individuals that wish to practice a certain profession or trade. Pursuant to this power, nearly every state in the country has enacted licensing laws for the funeral profession. Individuals seeking to hold themselves out to the public as funeral directors must achieve a certain educational level, undergo specialized training, and obtain licenses from the state. In order to retain the license, the funeral director must perform his duties in an ethical manner and conform with the many governmental regulations which the state imposes.

Although state legislatures enact the licensing laws and other statutes that govern the funeral profession, typically the legislature will delegate to an administrative agency the task of the day-to-day regulation. Thus, most states have boards of funeral directors and embalmers that oversee the licensing statutes, investigate and inspect funeral homes, and conduct enforcement actions against those in the profession not in compliance with the laws. State boards usually have a number of funeral directors on the board as well as members of the public that represent consumer interests.

In carrying out their regulatory tasks, state boards often are given power by the legislature to promulgate the administrative regulations. For example, the law may delegate to the state board the authority to designate what equipment a funeral home must have in order to receive a license. As long as the regulation promulgated by the board is within the delegation of power it has received from the legislature, the administrative regulation will generally be upheld by the courts.

b. *Case Law.*

Many of the principles that govern funeral law have their roots in the decisions of state and local courts. A court interprets the law and applies it to the facts of the case it is deciding. Therefore, once a law is enacted, it is up to the court to decide precisely what the legislature intended by enacting the law. The court construes the scope and applicability of the law to the facts before it.

Courts are occasionally called upon to decide the constitutionality of a statute or regulation. The state constitution is the primary law of each state. Therefore, if a statute violates a constitutional principle, it is struck down as unconstitutional. Similarly, if an administrative regulation exceeds the authority of the regulatory body promulgating it, it is declared void.

Once a particular issue is resolved by a court, a principle is established which will control future decisions by that court or lower courts. This is known as the doctrine of *stare decisis*. It means that a court deciding a point

2

gives to precedent the authority of established law. Absent some other conditions or a changed attitude on the part of the court, the doctrine will be followed and the preceding decision will control the ruling in the new case.

Courts of equity have the authority to settle controversies concerning dead bodies. A court of equity is one that has the authority to issue injunctions and other mandatory directions which parties must follow. For example, if a family were having a dispute regarding the final disposition of a body, they would apply to a court of equity to adjudicate the dispute and order the proper resolution.

c. Common Law.

Not all law is codified in statutes and regulations. There is a great body of unwritten law that is referred to as the "common law". The common law consists of maxims, principles, and judicial decisions that have been passed down from hundreds of years of jurisprudence. Much of the common law has its roots in English and early colonial law.

The common law fills up gaps in our legal system. It provides most of the principles that govern our basic rights as members of society. Therefore, it is not surprising that many aspects of funeral law are impacted by the common law. For example, the establishment of whom is given the right to take possession of the body upon death and direct its ultimate disposition has its roots in the common law.

d. Federal Law.

Prior to 1980, funeral law was generated primarily by state legislatures and judicial decisions by state and local courts. These sources, combined with the common law, govern nearly all aspects of the profession.

In the past fifteen years, the federal government has emerged as a major source of regulation for the funeral director. Some regulations, such as the Federal Trade Commission's Funeral Rule, are specific to funeral service; other statutes and regulations, such as the safety requirements of the Occupational Safety and Health Administration or the Americans with Disabilities Act cover many businesses.

The fact that over one-third of this book is now devoted solely to federal laws and regulations portrays the growing importance to the funeral industry of the federal government.

1.3   Obligations of the Funeral Professional

In the past fifteen years, the funeral director has come under a dizzying array of government regulations. Not surprisingly, this has placed the funeral director under even greater pressure in carrying out his or her duties.

The funeral directors that will be successful are those that see government regulation for what it is — a well-intentioned but often imperfect method to protect consumers and employees. Funeral directors who make a whole-hearted attempt to understand the laws and regulations and incorporate them into the funeral home business routine will often find means to soften the disruption caused by the regulation while improving upon its beneficial effects. For example, some funeral directors have reported that, in implementing the OSHA regulations discussed in Chapter Thirteen, they have taken steps beyond those required by the OSHA regulations to improve the safety of employees who work in the preparation room.

Implementations of the Americans with Disabilities Act standards (see Chapters Nine and Twelve) will undoubtedly cause some funeral directors, especially those in older buildings, to undertake expensive capital improvements. However, the elderly and disabled who arrange or attend funeral services in those facilities will greatly appreciate the funeral director's concern for their comfort. Although such benefits are intangible, funeral directors are well aware that a successful funeral operation is the direct result of the accumulation over the years of intangibles such as goodwill and trust. Families, even those that do not benefit directly from wheelchair ramps and accessible bathrooms, will take recognition of the funeral home's consideration for the disabled.

As is often heard these days, putting up with government regulation is one of the costs of doing business. However, the resourceful funeral director does not look upon government regulation as a burdensome cost. Rather, to him or her it is a challenge that, if understood and accepted, can be a tool for improving business and service to his or her clientele.

Chapter Two

DISPOSITION OF THE DEAD

2.1 Dead Body Defined

The term "dead body" means specifically the body of a human being deprived of life but not yet entirely disintegrated. The term "corpse" is a synonymous term with the term "dead body". A body to be legally a dead body or corpse must meet three conditions: it must be the body of a human being, without life, and not entirely disintegrated.

Given the advancements in technology in the past 30 years, society's definition of "death" is in flux. In the 1950 case of *Thomas v. Anderson*, 96 Cal. App. 2d 371, 215 P. 2d 478, the court stated that death occurs when life ceases, which takes place when the heart stops beating and respiration ends. In the 1979 case of *Lovats v. District Court*, 198 Col. 419, 601 P. 2d 1072, the court stated that for legal and medical purposes, an individual who has sustained irreversible cessation of all functioning of the brain, including the brain stem, is dead. With modern medical technology, this latter definition is becoming the most widely used, because a person's heart or lungs may continue to function through artificial means even though the person has no brain function.

Under the law, a dead body is a body that has not yet disintegrated. Therefore, a disintegrated corpse or the bones of a skeleton do not constitute a "dead body" in the eyes of the law. In *State v. Glass*, 27 O. App. 2d 214, 273 N.E. 2d 893, a real estate developer who had ordered bulldozers to level land upon which an old cemetery was located was charged with a violation of Ohio's "Grave Robbery" statute. The site that was developed contained the graves of three persons buried about 120 years earlier. In reversing the conviction of the developer, the Appeals Court stated as follows:

> "A cadaver is not an everlasting thing. After undergoing an
> undefined degree of decomposition, it ceases to be a dead
> body in the eyes of the law."

2.2 Legal Status of a Dead Body

For over one thousand years, the courts have struggled over whether a dead body does or does not constitute property. In early English law, it was established that the dead body was within the exclusive control of the Church. From this notion, courts developed the principle that no individual had property rights in the dead body. Thus, it was said that a dead body is the property of no one and there is no property in a dead body.

As the law became more secular, courts began to acknowledge that the surviving spouse and next of kin do have a right to take possession of the body to arrange its disposition. While the courts stopped short of declaring that a dead body was the "property" of the surviving family member, it recognized that survivors had quasi-property rights in the dead body.

One of the more scholarly analysis of this quasi-property right is found in the decision of the U.S. Sixth Circuit Court of Appeals in *Brotherton v. Cleveland*, 923 F.2d 477 (6th Cir. 1991). In that case, a surviving spouse sued the county coroner for removing her deceased husband's corneas without her consent. The court was faced with the issue of whether the spouse had been deprived of property without the due process of law.

The coroner's office maintained that the dead body was not property, and therefore, the spouse had no property rights to the corneas. The Court of Appeals refused to adopt the coroner's narrow interpretation. Rather, it analyzed exactly what "property" is:

> "The concept of 'property' in the law is extremely broad and abstract. The legal definition of 'property' most often refers not to a particular physical object, but rather to the legal bundle of rights recognized in that object. Thus, 'property' is often conceptualized as a 'bundle of rights.' The 'bundle of rights' which have been associated with property include the right to possess, to use, to exclude, to profit, and to dispose."

Finding that American courts had rejected early English law and had recognized that the next of kin has a quasi-property right in the decedent's body for the purpose of disposition, the court held that the spouse had a possessory right to the body and that the coroner's taking of the corneas violated that right.

The court's decision in *Brotherton* is consistent with the prevailing view of the dead body as "quasi-property." It is not property in the commercial sense, but the law does provide a bundle of rights to the next of kin in relation to that body. The survivor is given the right to take the body for purposes of disposition, to allow body parts to be used within the confines of the law, to exclude others from possession of the body, and to dispose of the body. This bundle of rights renders the dead body the quasi-property of the surviving family member.

2.3   Necessity of Disposition

It is well within the police powers of the government to require the orderly disposition of the dead in order to promote public health. Society has recognized that health and safety concerns, as well as public morality, necessitate the disposition of the dead by regulated methods. Courts have regularly upheld criminal statutes requiring the proper disposition of the dead. In *State v. Robinson*, 202 Neb. 210, 274 N.E. 2d 553 (1979), an individual had placed a dead body in the trunk of a car and then abandoned the automobile. He was convicted under a Nebraska statute making it a criminal offense for any person to throw away or abandon any dead human body, or any portion thereof, in any place other than a regular place for burial and under properly issued death certificates. The Nebraska Supreme Court upheld the constitutionality of the criminal statute.

Statutes which impose criminal penalties for the failure to bury or incinerate a corpse within a reasonable time after death have been applied to funeral directors. In two New York cases, (*People ex rel. Travis v. Daniels*, 57 NYS 2d 457 (1945); *People v. Ackley*, 62 NYS 2d 771 (1946)) funeral directors who had accepted bodies but failed to see to their proper disposition were held to be criminally liable.

2.4   Methods of Disposition

In the United States, there are a number of lawful methods of disposition of a dead body. Certainly, the most common is in-ground burial. Provided that the burial is on property dedicated as a public or private cemetery, it is lawful. In some rural areas, burial may be on private property, although the family may have to dedicate it as a family cemetery. Entombment may also be above ground where the body is placed in a mausoleum. In rare cases, such as Mao's tomb in China, the body will be indefinitely preserved for viewing.

As noted in Chapter Seven, cremation has gained wide acceptance in the United States as a method of disposition. Although cremation has been used for thousands of years by many cultures, it was infrequently utilized in the United States until the last fifty years. Provided the crematory is properly licensed and in compliance with state and local laws, the cremation of bodies is a perfectly legal form of disposition.

It must be noted that cremation is not technically a method of disposition, but actually one step in a mode of disposition. After the cremation, cremains will be collected and placed in an urn. Those cremains may be retained by the family, placed in a niche in a columbarium, entombed in a cemetery, or scattered. The scattering of cremains is usually confined to scattering gardens in cemeteries or at open sea. As cremation has become more popular, the Government has restricted the scattering of cremains in public places and some inland waterways. Scattering of cremains in the ocean may be made at a distance of three nautical miles from the shoreline. Reports of the scattering must be filed with the Environmental Protection Agency.

An infrequent method of disposition of the dead occurs in the case of death at sea. Under Maritime Law, the captain of a ship on the high seas is invested with authority and responsibility for the health and safety of the crew and passengers. When a person dies aboard ship, the captain, if he deems it necessary for the safety of the crew and passengers, may order the body cast into the sea.

In *Brambir v. Cunard White Star Ltd.*, 37 F. Sup. 906 (1941), plaintiff's husband died on a voyage from Liverpool to New York. He was buried at sea six days prior to the ship landing in New York. The widow sued the shipping lines because it had not embalmed the body or notified the widow. In dismissing the complaint, the court held as follows:

> "A person who books passage on an ocean going steamer impliedly acquiesces to be bound by the custom of the sea and consents to burial therein in the event of death during the voyage."

Burial at sea is also sometimes desired when a death takes place on land. Generally, no such burials are permitted on in-land waterways. Burial at sea may take place in the ocean at a distance of at least three nautical miles from the shoreline. In some designated areas, there are requirements on the depth of the water. Additionally, the body must be properly weighted in a special shroud to insure that the remains sink to the bottom rapidly and permanently. Reports of all such burials must be made to the Environmental Protection Agency.

Another method of lawful disposition is the donation of the body to medical science. Because medical science requires dead body for dissection and study, each state in the country allows by statute for a decedent or a decedent's survivors to make a gift of decedent's body to medical science. The Uniform Anatomical Gift Act is discussed in greater detail in Chapter Four.

Chapter Three

RIGHTS OF PARTIES UNDERTAKING DISPOSITION

3.1 In General

The party who legally undertakes to dispose of a dead body is vested with certain rights and charged with certain duties ... rights and duties granted and imposed by law for the protection of the decedent's survivors and for the protection of the public. This paramount right to arrange the disposition of a dead body would indeed be empty and meaningless without a grant of certain specific rights necessary to effect disposition free from interference from others.

3.2 Right of Custody

A dead body is not property in the ordinary sense of the word, but it is a tangible object over which dominion is granted to the party undertaking the disposition. However, that right of custody is not absolute. Rather, it is a limited right, given for a specific purpose, and subject to revocation if the party possessing it does not utilize it for a proper purpose. As stated by the Court in the case of *Pierce v. Proprietors of the Swan Point Cemetery*, 10 R.I. 227:

> "Although as we have said the body is not property in the usually recognized sense of the word, yet we may consider it as a sort of quasi-property to which certain persons may have rights, as they have duties to perform toward it, arising out of our common humanity. But the person having charge of it cannot be considered as the owner of it in any sense whatever; he holds it only as a sacred trust for the benefit of all who may from family or friendship have an interest in it, and we think that a court of equity may regulate it as such and change the custody if improperly managed."

The person exercising the right of disposition is granted the right to take possession and control of the body. The possession may be actual or constructive —actual possession where the body is physically within his custody and constructive possession where the body is physically in the custody of another. Thus, where the body is at the home of the next of kin, the possession is actual; where the body is at a hospital or mortuary, the custody of the next of kin is said to be constructive.

Custody of a dead body may be had only for the purpose of disposing of it in the proper manner. As seen in Chapter Two, the failure to dispose of the body in a lawful manner not only takes away an individual's right of custody, but also can lead to criminal sanctions against such individual.

Possession and control of the body attaches from the moment of death and it may be continued for a reasonable length of time. The reasonableness of the length of time during which a body may be held pending final disposal is to be determined by the circumstances of the case. In the usual case several days may suffice. Under a different set of facts it may be necessary to withhold disposition for a longer time and such delay is not unwarranted where the cause is justifiable. In the case of death by contagious disease, however, the law may stipulate the maximum time during which the body may be held. In such cases the rule of reason is abrogated by the statutory provisions.

3.3   Right to Control the Funeral

The individual undertaking disposition has the power to exercise control over all matters relating to the funeral. He is free to choose whether to use a funeral director, which funeral director to use, what type of service, if any, will be held, what funeral merchandise will be purchased, and what the eventual method of disposition will be. In addition, the individual may arrange the time and place of burial convenient to himself and disregard the feelings of others. In this respect, he is subject only to the regulations and rules of the crematory or cemetery.

The right to arrange the disposition is an exclusive right. In other words, if an individual has the paramount right of disposition, he is not compelled by law to share it with others. This being the case, the individual may elect to hold a private funeral and invite or exclude those who he chooses.

For example, in the case of *Rader v. Davis*, 154 Iowa 306, 134 N.W. 849 (1912), a husband and wife had been divorced. The custody of the couple's only child was granted exclusively to the wife. When the child died the wife refused to allow the husband to attend the funeral. The court upheld the wife's decision to exclude the husband, stating in part:

> "There was no duty, as we understand it, however, to conduct a public funeral, and if there were, private funerals are so common in this country that we would not feel disposed to say that public services are required to be held…There is no implied invitation to anyone to attend a funeral conducted from a private dwelling unless it be announced that such funeral is public, and even is so an-

10

nounced, the invitation may be revoked and anyone denied the right to attend whose presence might be objectionable."

The courts have made clear that the right to exclude others from the funeral extends even to services conducted in cemeteries. In *Ross v. Forest Lawn Memorial Park*, 199 Cal. Rptr. 854 (1984), the facts showed that the mother of the decedent instructed the cemetery that the funeral was to be restricted to invited guests only. The mother was especially concerned that unruly companions of her deceased 17 year old daughter would disturb the funeral. The cemetery orally agreed to take all reasonable steps to comply with the mother's request.

The funeral ceremony was completely disrupted by the decedent's friends. They attended the chapel services and the graveside services in outlandish outfits, which the Court described as "not in accord with traditional funeral attire." During the services, they drank and used cocaine, physically and verbally abused guests, and created a disturbance which had to be settled by the police. The mother sued the cemetery alleging negligence and breach of contract and claiming damages for mental and emotional distress.

The California Court of Appeals upheld the validity of the mother's complaint. The Court first noted that the mother, as next of kin to the daughter (the daughter had no spouse or children), had the right of disposition. The right of disposition, according to the Court, included "the right to determine the time, manner and place of burial." The Court then examined case law from other jurisdictions and concluded the right to determine the "manner" of burial gave the mother the right to exclude others from the funeral. In reaching this decision, the Appellate Court cited *Haney v. Stamper*, 277 Ky 1, 125 S.W. 2d 761 (1939), wherein it was held that a widow could rightfully exclude the decedent's brother from the funeral.

Since the mother had the right to exclude others from the funeral and since the cemetery had agreed to take steps to honor her wishes, the failure of the cemetery to take those steps constituted a breach of contract. Moreover, because the cemetery was aware that its failure to exclude the uninvited friends would cause mental and emotional injury to the mother, she could collect damages for her mental suffering.

The individual arranging the funeral may notify relatives and others at his will or he may elect not to do so. In *Seaton v. Commonwealth*, 149 Ky 498, 149 S.W. 871 (1912), the issue was addressed by the Court as follows:

"Is appellate (the defendant) subject to punishment because he refused to permit his relatives and those of his wife or others to be notified so that they might be present

11

at the interment? His relatives and friends may have regarded this conduct on his part as lack of consideration or respect for their feelings in the matter, but this is the extent of the bearing which his conduct in this particular can have upon the case. They have no legal right to be present. They may have been offended because not notified or invited, but no ground of complaint is afforded to the public on this account. In some localities funerals are not infrequently attended by invitations. Some are strictly private; while others are open to the public. Those are matters which address themselves to the discretion and will of those interested . . . the relatives and friends of the deceased."

3.4   Right to Choose Disposition

The paramount right to take custody of the body includes the right to choose the method of disposition. Therefore, the person found to have the paramount right has unfettered discretion in selecting if the decedent will be buried, cremated, or disposed of by some other method.

In *Dumouchelle v. Duke University*, 317 S.E. 2d 100 (N.C. App. 1984), the next of kin elected to have the decedent cremated. However, the executor of the decedent's will, noting that the will had expressed decedent's wish to buried in Ohio, countermanded the cremation order and had the decedent interred in Ohio. When the next of kin sued, the court held that, given the decedent's instruction in the will, the executor had the paramount right to arrange the disposition. This being the case, his decision to bury the body rather than cremate it was well within his right.

3.5   Funeral Director with Right of Disposition

The lawful rights of the funeral director undertaking a funeral are primarily derived from two sources. There are those rights which are granted and imposed by statute and those arising from the funeral contract.

The former consists of those rights defined and provided by the statutes, ordinances and regulations of the jurisdiction where the funeral director practices. These are the laws and licensing regulations which authorize the funeral director to practice his profession. Generally, they empower him to take those actions which are incident to the funeral, i.e. transporting the dead, embalming, conducting funeral services, and arranging dispositions in cemeteries or crematories.

The second source of the funeral director's authority arises from the contract entered into between the funeral director and the individual with the

12

paramount right of disposition. The funeral director has no rights in his professional capacity with respect to a dead body until such time as a valid contract is entered into between himself and another, either expressly or implicitly.

3.6 Funeral Contract

a. In General.

The funeral contract is an agreement between a funeral director and another competent party of legal age, whereby the consumer purchases, and the funeral director agrees to furnish merchandise and services. The funeral contract may be oral or written. When the contract is oral, it may be expressed or implied. For example, when an individual dies in a nursing home and the family has left instructions to call a particular funeral home, that funeral home has an implied contract with that family to conduct the removal of the body.

The contract may be between the funeral home and the decedent's estate, his family, and/or an unrelated third party. Since, as will be discussed in Chapter Six, the decedent's estate is generally responsible for the decedent's funeral bill, it is an implied party to the contract. Funeral directors will often have the next of kin or surviving spouses execute the funeral contract also to show that the funeral home has authority to conduct the contracted services and to provide another source of payment in the event the estate is insolvent. Third parties that are unrelated to the decedent may also arrange for the funeral such as employers, the armed forces, or government welfare agencies.

b. Disclosures.

In addition to the disclosures required by the FTC Funeral Rule (see Chapter Fourteen) and the Truth-In-Lending provisions (see Chapter Fifteen), some states have laws and regulations requiring that certain written disclosures must be given to the person making funeral arrangements. Generally, these disclosures are as follows: 1) the price of the funeral and a list of all services and merchandise included in the funeral; 2) the price of each supplemental item of service or merchandise; 3) a list of the cash advances made by the funeral director on behalf of the person making the funeral arrangements; and 4) the method of payment.

In states with these requirements, the funeral director may not simply enter into an oral funeral contract with the other party, but is required to give a written memorandum of the transaction. These disclosures are intended to be in the best interest of the consumer, but are also beneficial to the funeral director — the written contract is legally more sound, is explicit as to method of payment, is easier to prove in the case of default by the purchaser, and is proof of a valid contract.

c. Contract Terminology.

To insure that the contract is enforceable and in accordance with the state law prescribing certain disclosures and proscribing certain practices, the funeral directors should use a contract form that has been reviewed and approved by legal counsel. This section describes provisions which are typically included in a standard funeral contract:

(1) **Itemization.** The FTC Funeral Rule requires price itemization of the components of the funeral services (i.e. the goods and services purchased). Some states also have statutes or rules requiring price itemization of funeral contracts. Therefore, the majority of the contract will spell out the goods and services purchased by the consumer.

(2) **Cash Transaction.** The funeral home should stipulate in the contract that the sale is a cash transaction and not a credit transaction. Credit transactions involve many disclosures, which need not be made if the funeral director does not qualify as a creditor as defined in the Truth-In-Lending provisions.

(3) **Late Payment Charge or Penalty Charge.** A funeral home may charge a late payment charge or penalty charge for unanticipated late payment. If this charge is imposed, state law should be reviewed to determine if any ceiling to the penalty applies. An example of the penalty clause is as follows: This is a CASH transaction due in full on (date) and without exception becomes past due and delinquent on the due date. A penalty of _____% per month (_____% per annum) on the unpaid balance for the unanticipated late payment will be charged effective (date).

(4) **Collection Fees.** A contract may stipulate that in the event of default, the undersigned (person or persons making the funeral arrangements) agree to pay all cost of collection including reasonable attorney's fees. State law should be consulted to insure that a collection provision is permissible.

(5) **Estate Liability.** In many states the primary liability for payment of a funeral bill is the estate of the decedent. (See Chapter Six). A funeral contract should include a statement that the undersigned is liable for payment of the funeral contract in addition to the liability imposed by law upon the estate. By doing this, the undersigned will be held responsible for payment in the event the estate is insolvent. Also, funeral homes may charge a late payment fee as stipulated in the contract even though the estate is liable for the payment of the contract. This charge could be substantial because many times payment is held up for many months on account of the administration of the estate.

(6) **Joint and Several (Individual) Liability.** Directly above the signature line designated for the signature(s) of the person(s) making the funeral arrangements, the funeral home should include a statement similar to the one that follows: "I/we the undersigned, severally and jointly, hereby authorize the above funeral contract and promise to make payment thereof." With this statement the funeral home is holding the persons jointly and individually liable for the payment of the funeral bill.

(7) **Disclaimer of Warranties.** A funeral contract may include a disclaimer of the implied warranties of merchantability and fitness for a particular purpose. These implied warranties basically mean that the casket and other goods sold will fulfill their intended uses, e.g. that the casket will be sufficiently strong to hold the body and allow the body to be transported. If the bottom of the casket falls out, the warranty has been breached and the funeral director will be liable for damages.

To avoid liability for implied warranties, funeral directors may disclaim the warranties. The following statement may be used by the funeral director as a disclaimer of impled and expressed warranties:

"DISCLAIMER OF WARRANTIES

THE _____ FUNERAL HOME MAKES NO REPRESENTATIONS OR WARRANTIES REGARDING THE MERCHANDISE SOLD WITH THIS FUNERAL SERVICE. THE ONLY WARRANTIES, EXPRESSED OR IMPLIED, GRANTED IN CONNECTION WITH THE MERCHANDISE SOLD WITH THIS FUNERAL SERVICE ARE THE EXPRESS WRITTEN WARRANTIES, IF ANY, EXTENDED BY THE MANUFACTURERS THEREOF. NO OTHER WARRANTIES, EXPRESSED OR IMPLIED, INCLUDING THE IMPLIED WARRANTIES OF MERCHANTABILITY OR FITNESS FOR A PARTICULAR PURPOSE, ARE EXTENDED BY THE FUNERAL HOME."

Prior to disclaiming these warranties, funeral directors should consult state law to ensure that such a disclaimer is permissible. In some states, it is against the law to disclaim implied warranties given to consumers.

Many of the caskets and vaults sold by funeral directors have been warranted by the manufacturers of those caskets and vaults. While these warranties are extended to the consumers, funeral directors should ensure that consumers understand that the warranties are made by the manufacturer and not by the funeral home.

Chapter Four

WHO HAS THE RIGHT OF DISPOSITION

4.1   Introduction

As seen the previous chapter, the paramount right of disposition provides an individual with broad authority in regard to the funeral and ultimate
disposition of a dead body. What has not been addressed up to this point,
however, is who is given this power. This is an issue of critical importance for
the funeral director who will from time-to-time encounter family members in
dispute as to the funeral and final disposition of a decedent. While generally
the funeral director should not undertake to make legal decisions as to who
has the paramount right of disposition, it is imperative that he have a firm
understanding of this issue to avoid possible legal liability for improperly complying with the instructions of one who did not have the paramount right of
disposition.

4.2   General Rule of Priority

Unfortunately, for the funeral director there is not, in most states, an
iron-clad rule of whom is given the paramount right of disposition. There is a
well-recognized order of priority, but it is subject to so many exceptions that it
would be inadvisable for the funeral director to simply adhere to the rule
when deciding which family member has the right of disposition.

The general rule, as stated in the landmark case of *Pettigrew v. Pettigrew*,
207 Pa. 313, 56 A. 878 (1904), is as follows:

> "The result of a full examination of the subject is that there
> is no universal rule applicable alike to all cases. But each
> must be considered in equity on its own merits, having
> due regard for the interest of the public, the wishes of the
> decedent and the rights and feelings of those entitled to
> be heard by reason or relation or association. Subject to
> this general result, it may be laid down first that the para-
> mount right is in the surviving husband or widow, and if the
> parties were living in the normal relations of marriage it
> will require a very strong case to justify a court in interfer-
> ing with the wish of the survivor. Secondly, if there is no
> surviving husband or widow the right is in the next of kin in
> order of their relation to the decedent, as children of proper

17

age, parents, brothers, sisters or more distant kin modified by circumstances of public intimacy or association with the decedent. Thirdly, how far the desires of the decedent should prevail against those of the surviving husband or wife is an open question, but as against the remoter connections such wishes, strongly or recently expressed, should usually prevail."

While the decision in *Pettigrew* recited the well-recognized rule that the paramount right of disposition goes first to the surviving spouse, then to the children of legal age of the decedent, then to the decedent's parents, and then to the decedent's brothers and sisters, the crucial teaching of *Pettigrew* is that each case must be decided on its own particular facts.

Except in those few states which have established statutes on this issue, most courts will look at the general rule for guidance, but also to such factors as the wishes of the decedent, whether any parties waived their rights, what relatives were living with and/or supporting the decedent at the time of death, and other factors particular to each case. Further complicating this issue is the fact that some states give great weight to factors such as the wishes of the decedent while other states will treat such wishes as just another element that the court shall weigh in deciding who has the right of disposition.

It is against this background that this chapter reviews the general rule of priority and the factors that courts will examine. However, the overriding consideration for the funeral director to remember is that these decisions should be left up to a court of law and should not be made by the funeral director.

4.3   Important Factors Affecting General Rule

As just reviewed, the general rule is that the surviving spouse has the primary right of disposition and, in the absence of a surviving spouse, the right is given to the next of kin. The designation of next of kin follows the blood line with adult children being the nearest in degree, followed by parents, and then brothers and sisters of the decedent.

The general rule of priority, however, is subject to a number of factors, the most important of which are as follows:

a. *Wishes of the Decedent.*

By far the most important factor in determining whether to follow the general rule is the express preference of the decedent. In some states, the preference of the decedent is paramount, superseding even the contrary wishes of the surviving spouse. In most other states the preference of the decedent is entitled to significant weight in balancing all the factors to be considered.

As indicated by most judicial decisions in this area, each case turns on its own particular facts. Thus, in deciding how much weight to give the decedent's preference, a court will look at a number of particular elements. One of the most critical is the mental capacity of the decedent at the time the preference was voiced. Secondly, courts examine the proximity of the expression of preference to the time of death. If the preference was expressed in close proximity to death, courts will give it greater weight than if the preference is made years prior to death.

The form of the preference is usually not important to the court. In other words, whether the preference was made orally or in writing is not decisive. While some courts will attach special significance to a preference written in a will, most courts do not.

Of course, the courts will balance the decedent's preferences against the contrary wishes of other relatives. Certainly, the most problematical case is when the decedent's preferences are not in accord with the surviving spouse's. Jurisdictions are fairly split on this issue with some courts following the decedent's wishes and others holding that the surviving spouse's rights cannot be defeated. Often in deciding this issue, courts will look to see whether there was any estrangement between the couple prior to death.

In balancing the decedent's preferences against that of the next of kin, some courts tend to be more willing to side with the decedent's preferences. For example, in *Dumouchille v. Duke University*, 317 S.E. 2d 100, (N.C. App. 1984), the children of the decedent wished to have the body cremated. However, in the decedent's will, the executor was instructed to arrange burial in Ohio. Although the North Carolina Court of Appeals acknowledged that the right of possession of the body for purposes of disposition normally belongs to the next of kin, it held that rule was superseded when there was a testamentary provision governing burial. Therefore, the funeral instructions of the decedent took precedence over the wishes of the next of kin.

b. *Special Relationship.*

Another factor courts will examine is whether there are any special relationships between relatives and the decedent. Factors such as living under the same roof, financial support, or a special intimacy between the decedent and a relative may persuade the court to grant that relative the right of disposition.

19

The existence of special relationships can be especially important when individuals who share the right of disposition disagree on the funeral. In those cases, the courts may side with the individual who had a closer relationship with the decedent. For example, in a dispute among adult children, the court may give the right to the adult child that lived under the same roof or provided financial support to the deceased parent. Similarly, in the case of a death of a child of divorced parents, courts will usually give the right of disposition to that parent that had custody of the child.

c. Waiver.

Courts have recognized that the individual with a paramount right of disposition who does not take action to arrange the disposition may waive the paramount right. For example, in the *Rauhe v. Langeland Chapel*, 44 Mich. App. 371, 265 N.W. 2d 313 (1973), a mother decided not to have a funeral for her deceased son and instead donated the body to medical science. The body was lost while being transported to the medical facility. When the mother sued, the court dismissed her claim ruling that she had relinquished her paramount right to direct the disposition.

4.4   Statutory Exceptions to the General Rule of Priority

Because of the uncertainty in this area and given the many types of relationships that can be produced by multiple marriages and divorces, some states have attempted to address this issue by statute. But as with judicial decisions in this area, the states are not consistent on who should prevail in the case of a dispute between the surviving spouse and the contrary wishes of the decedent.

Of the handful of states that have passed laws in this area, some have elected to honor the wishes of the decedent. Thus, Washington's new law states that if the decedent has signed a written statement setting forth the place and method of disposition of his or her remains, and the document is witnessed, it constitutes a legal authorization for the funeral director to proceed without obtaining permission from relatives. In addition, if the decedent has entered into a prepaid preneed contract, family members cannot cancel or substantially change the contract. Funeral directors who rely upon the contract are granted immunity from lawsuits by relatives desiring a different disposition.

In Kansas and Illinois, new laws allow an individual to appoint an agent under a power of attorney for health care. Typically, an agent's authority to act for a principal terminates upon the death of the principal. However, in the Kansas and Illinois law, the agent is given authority to arrange for the disposition of the body of the principal. Moreover, the agent can make these decisions after the death of the principal and those decisions will be binding upon the contrary wishes of the surviving spouse or next of kin. Funeral directors that follow the wishes of the agent holding the power of attorney are immune from lawsuit.

Other states that have considered this issue have not gone as far as Washington, Kansas and Illinois. For example, New Jersey recently enacted a law which reaffirmed that the surviving spouse has the paramount right of disposition. However, the law does recognize that the decedent may provide other directions that will override the surviving spouse. Nevertheless, the law specifically provides that a preneed funeral contract entered into by the decedent does not constitute "other directions" for the purpose of overriding the contrary wishes of the spouse.

It is anticipated that more states will seek to address these issues by statute. Certainly, they will looking to see how these new statutes operate in Kansas, Illinois and Washington.

4.5   Anatomical Gift Act

In response to the need to promote organ donation and other anatomical gifts, the Uniform Anatomical Gift Act has been enacted in all fifty states and the District of Columbia. Since this statute is based upon a model law, most states have the identical statute. Some states have enacted minor changes to the Uniform Act.

The Act generally provides that any individual of sound mind and legal age may donate all or part of his body upon his death. The person may designate the gift in his Last Will and Testament. The gift is effective upon death without waiting for probate. If the will is invalid for any reason, the gift is valid to the extent it was acted upon in good faith.

A donation may also be made by a document other than a will. The document must be signed by the individual in the presence of two witnesses. Many states have a prescribed form for the gift. Also, many states have statutorily provided that a person may legally use the reverse side of a valid drivers license as a donation form.

In addition to the decedent, the Uniform Anatomical Gift Act also authorizes the surviving spouse and the next of kin to make donations of the decedent's body. As with the paramount right of disposition, there is a priority in who has the power to make a gift. The first priority is the surviving spouse, followed by the adult son or daughter, either parent, an adult brother or sister, a guardian of the decedent at the time of his death, or any other person authorized or under obligation to dispose of the body.

21

The relative may make a gift of all or part of the decedent's body if there are no contrary indications by the decedent or if there is no opposition by a member of the same class or a relative with a higher priority. In the event notice of these contrary indications or opposition have been given or is known by the donee, the donee may not accept the gift.

The gift may be made to any donee authorized by the Act to accept donations. These donees typically include hospitals, accredited medical or dental schools, surgeons, physicians, medical storage banks, and designated persons needing therapy or transplantations. The donee must employ the gift for medical or dental research, education or the advancement of medical science or therapy. Where the gift is of the entire body, the surviving spouse or next of kin may, subject to the terms of the gift, authorize embalming and the use of the body in a funeral service. Likewise, where the gift is a part of the body, the remainder may, after removal of the donated part, be delivered to the surviving spouse, next of kin or other person for disposition. The Act provides that any person acting in good faith compliance with the Act shall not be liable for damages in a civil action or subject to prosecution in a criminal action.

Unlike the issue regarding the paramount right of disposition, there is no question regarding the supremacy of a gift made under the Uniform Anatomical Gift Act. That donation takes precedence over any contrary wishes of the survivors. Provided that the gift has been made in compliance with the legal requirements of the Act, no relative can supersede the gift.

4.6   Duty of a Funeral Director in the Case of Conflict

Where the right of disposition is in question, it is the obligation of the funeral director to hold the body until the proper party authorizes its disposition. It is not for the funeral director to decide the question nor to attempt to influence the decision. Rather, when faced with a dispute among relatives, the funeral director should advise all concerned that he will not undertake any disposition until the parties have come to a settlement or until a court has issued final instructions as to what action should be taken.

Chapter Five

DUTIES OF THE FUNERAL DIRECTOR

5.1 In General

The funeral director in carrying out the preparation of the body and the direction of the funeral service is under various legal and contractual duties. The sources of these duties are the statutory laws of the state, the requirements of the funeral contract, and the common law. If the funeral director violates these duties, he will incur liability to the state and/or the family of the decedent.

5.2 Statutory Duties

a. Permits.

In nearly all jurisdictions, the funeral director is required to obtain permits from appropriate authorities to arrange for the proper disposition of the dead. Typically, this involves obtaining a death certificate, burial permit and transit permit. State and municipal statutes and regulations which require these permits have been upheld by courts as reasonable exercises by the state of its police power to protect the health of the public. In *Myers v. Clarke*, 122 Ky. 866, 90 S.W. 1049 (1906), the court found that a regulation of the municipal Department of Health requiring a burial permit to be issued before a decedent could be interred was a reasonable measure to prevent the spread of contagious diseases in the city and to protect the general health of the inhabitants.

Several states have adopted a uniform certificate of death and burial permit for the purpose of recording death and burial officially. The mechanics and contents of these permits are not within the province of this volume.

b. Health Laws and Regulations.

There are a number of statutes and health regulations which regulate the practice of embalming and funeral directing, some of which are discussed in later chapters of this volume. However, with regard to the proper handling, preparation and burial of bodies, the funeral director will have to be aware of the relevant statutes and regulations in his jurisdiction. States and municipalities differ widely in the regulation of embalming and burial.

For example, most states require embalming if the body is to be involved in interstate transportation. Some states provide for embalming in the event of death by contagious disease and other states require embalming if

23

burial or cremation is not to take place within a certain time frame. These are a few states, such as Texas, where the law never requires embalming. The funeral director must, of course, be completely cognizant of these laws not only to maintain compliance with state and local law, but to properly represent to funeral consumers what the law does and does not require with regard to embalming, burial and cremation.

5.3   Contractual Obligations

When the funeral director enters into the funeral contract, whether oral or written, he promises to undertake certain obligations. If he breaches these obligations, he is liable for the damages that flow as a result of his breach. These damages, more often than not, involve the emotional distress that can result to survivors when the services of the funeral director are not carried out as promised. The recovery of these damages is discussed more fully in Section 5.5 on mental anguish.

The funeral contract imposes numerous duties on the funeral director, some implied and others expressed. Although it is not possible to detail all of the possible contractual breaches that can arise, the student of mortuary law should be familiar with the following breaches which often may end up in litigation.

   a.   *Negligent Embalming.*

When a funeral director contracts to embalm a body, he undertakes to use the skill and care of a reasonably prudent and careful man skilled in the art of embalming. If the embalming falls short of that standard of care, the funeral director will be liable for the damages that result therefrom.

For example, in *Thompson v. the Duncan Bros. Funeral Homes, Inc.*, 116 Misc.2d 227, 445 N.Y.S.2d 324 (1982), the casket was opened for the family and the remains were found to be decomposed, swollen, odoriferous and leaking fluid. The court awarded members of the family $35,000.00 to compensate them for the personal injuries they suffered upon witnessing the results of the negligent embalming.

In a California case, a funeral home was held liable for the alleged negligent embalming of the plaintiff's father. In this case, the decedent's body was shipped from California to Oklahoma. Upon arrival in Oklahoma, the body was "in a decayed condition, malodorous and dripping fluid." The court held that "the mental and emotional shock suffered by the plaintiffs upon learning that the body was in such a condition made them ill, (and was) an element of compensable injury." *Carey v. Lima, Salmon and Tully Mortuary*, 168 Cal.App.2d 42, 335 P.2d 181, 182 (1959).

b. Negligent Funeral Directing.

The failure of a funeral director to perform the many duties involved in directing the funeral service will give rise to liability. In *Golston v. Lincoln Cemetery, Inc.*, 573 S.W.2d 700 (1978 Mo.App.), a funeral director who had failed to properly supervise the burial at the cemetery, thereby permitting the decedent to be buried in a shallow grave and without the vault that the contract provided for, was held liable for breach of contract. The court not only awarded damages for mental anguish suffered by the family, but also imposed punitive damages against the funeral director.

Similarly, in *Wilson v. Ferguson*, 747 S.W. 2d 499 (Tex. Ap. 1988), the facts showed that when the funeral procession arrived for the graveside ceremony, the grave had not been properly prepared. Rather than assisting the family, the funeral home employees "left the gravesite saying they were in a hurry for another funeral." When the body was later damaged at the cemetery, the court held that the funeral home had breached its contractual duty to perform its services with ordinary care.

In *Lamm v. Shingleton*, 231 N.C. 1, 55 S.E.2d 810 (1949), a funeral director was held liable for the mental distress suffered by a surviving spouse upon learning that mud and water had entered into a vault containing her husband's casket. The vault had leaked because the funeral director had failed to properly lock the vault.

In *Clark v. Smith*, 494 S.W.2d 192 (Tex. 1973), the employee of the defendant was instructed by the plaintiffs to hold the dead body until they decided what funeral director to call. When the defendant had possession of the body, it underwent drastic putrefactive changes. Although the defendant was never instructed to embalm the body, there was explicit testimony that he should take the body and keep it in a suitable condition pending burial. The plaintiffs brought suit for mental anguish suffered at the appearance of the decedent as a result of defendant's negligence in not keeping the body suitable for burial, in not using preservative fluids, in not refrigerating the body in order to preserve it, and in not informing the plaintiffs as to what was necessary to preserve the body to keep it suitable for a decent burial, all of which were proximate causes of plaintiffs' mental anguish. The court held that the above allegations constituted negligent breaches of a duty owed by the funeral director to the decedent's family.

Funeral directors may also be liable for failure to honor requests made by the family. For example, in *Meyer v. Nottger*, 241 N.W.2d 911 (Iowa 1976), the complaint alleged, among other things, that the funeral director had improperly refused to allow the plaintiffs to view the body and had failed to comply with his agreement to delay the funeral procession until the plaintiffs could arrive at the funeral. As a result, the plaintiffs were unable to attend the burial which they alleged resulted in mental anguish and, in one case, a heart attack. The court found that these allegations were legally sufficient to allow a jury to decide the case.

Substantial liability can be imposed for what appears to be minor errors of judgment. In a recent Washington case, the surviving spouse had requested that her husband be buried wearing his favorite cowboy hat. When the funeral director returned the hat to a different relative rather than complying with the request, the jury awarded the spouse $100,000.

c. Safeguard the Body.

Although cases of mentally deranged people sexually assaulting or harming bodies are rare occurrences, a funeral home may be liable for such generally unforeseen occurrences if it does not take reasonable precaution to safeguard the body. In *Draper Mortuary v. Superior Court*, 135 Cal.App.3d 533, 185 Cal.Rptr. 396 (1982), a person entered through an unlocked chapel door and sexually assaulted the body which was lying in state. Although the defendant claimed there was no history of such prior occurrences which would have forewarned him to take safeguards against such intrusions, the court rejected that defense and found the funeral home liable for violating its special duty of care that exists between a mortuary and a bereaved family who leaves the remains of their loved one in the care and custody of the funeral home.

d. Privacy.

If funeral directors fail to comply with the survivor's requests for confidentiality regarding the death or for privacy during the funeral arrangements, they can be held liable for breach of contract. In *Fitzsimmons v. Olinger Mortuary Ass'n*, 91 Colo. 544, 17 P.2d 535 (1932), a funeral director was requested to transport a body and prepare it for burial without any undue publicity. When the funeral director photographed the body and used it in advertisement, the court held that the funeral director had violated an expressed and implied promise not to violate the confidentiality of the family. The fact that the court found a violation of an implied promise suggests that the funeral director would have been liable for violating the confidentiality of the family even had the family not requested that the funeral director avoid any undue publicity.

The courts have also upheld a family's right to request a cemetery and presumably a funeral director, to exclude unwanted visitors from the funeral and burial. In *Ross v. Forest Lawn Memorial Park*, 199 Cal. Rptr. 854 (1984), the family had requested the cemetery to take appropriate measures to keep the graveside service private and to exclude a certain group of unwanted friends of the decedent. When the cemetery failed to take the appropriate measures and the graveside service was interrupted by the unwanted friends, the cemetery was held liable for breach of contract and the damages which resulted therefrom.

e. Defective Merchandise.

Funeral directors, as purveyors of merchandise, are held to the same implied warranties that other merchants are. By law these implied warranties, which include the implied warranties of "merchantability" and "fitness for a particular purpose," involve promises that the products are fit for the ordinary and particular purpose for which such goods are used. Unless these warranties are properly disclaimed (see Sections 3.6 and 15.3), the funeral director will be liable if the merchandise, e.g. caskets and vaults, prove defective.

For example, in *Estate of Harper v. Orlando Funeral Home, Inc.*, 366 So.2d 126 (Fla. App. 1979), a funeral director was held to have breached an implied warranty of merchantability and fitness for a particular purpose when a casket holding the body fell apart as it was being transported to the grave. Likewise, in *McDaniel v. Bass-Smith Funeral Home, Inc.*, 80 N.C. App. 629, 343 S.E.2d 228 (1986), a funeral home was found liable for supplying a casket that would not properly close. The evidence of the unworkmanlike condition was supported by findings that defendant's employees experienced difficulty closing the casket before funeral services and that one corner of the casket was not closed during the services, thereby allowing the deceased's remains to be visible. The court allowed the plaintiff to recover for emotional anguish under these facts.

In *Cottom v. McGuire Funeral Service, Inc.*, 262 A.2d 807 (D.C. 1970), a handle fell off a casket while it was being carried by a pallbearer. He was injured as a result and sued the funeral director alleging that the casket was defective. The lower court dismissed the complaint because it found that the pallbearer was not the intended "user" of the product and, therefore, the funeral director owed him no duty of care to provide a safe product. The Appellate Court reversed, however, and held that the pallbearer was indeed the intended "user" of the casket. The funeral director was held liable for supplying a defective product which violated the implied warranties of merchantability and fitness for a particular purpose.

f. Transportation.

A funeral home supplying the hearse and limousine for the conveyance of the body and the mourners respectively is a private carrier and, as such, is charged with the legal duty to transport its passengers in a safe and non-negligent manner. If the funeral home fails to exercise ordinary care in carrying out the transportation and, as a result thereof, a passenger is injured, the funeral home will be liable for breach of contract.

In order for the funeral home to be liable, it is necessary to show the negligent driver of the vehicle was an agent of the funeral home. In other words, if the driver is an employee of the funeral home or if the funeral home engages a limousine service and represents such cars to be owned by the funeral home, it will be liable for the negligence of such drivers. In *Sack v. A. R. Nunn & Son*, 129 O.S. 128 (1934), the Supreme Court of Ohio held that a funeral director who had undertaken by contract to transport a family could not relieve himself from the negligence of the driver by showing that he engaged another to perform the transportation , especially when the family had no notice that the transportation service was being rendered by someone other than the funeral director or one under his control.

On the other hand, if there is no agency relationship between the driver and the funeral director, liability will not be imposed. In *Pantall v. Schriver*, 135 O.S. 164 (1939), a volunteer driving his own vehicle in a funeral procession caused injury to his passengers due to negligence. The court relieved the funeral director of any liability because there was no showing that the negligent driver was under the control or direction of the funeral director.

g. *Aftercare.*

Aftercare refers to grief counselling, support groups, or other grief facilitation activities sponsored by funeral homes. In the past ten years, many funeral directors have begun programs in this very worthwhile and valuable service.

While no cases have been brought against funeral homes arising out of aftercare activities, there is a risk of some type of malpractice action. Similar claims have been brought against priests and ministers who attempt to counsel individuals and failed to recognize suicidal tendencies. For example, in *Nally v. Grace Community Church*, 157 Cal. App. 3d 912 (1984), the court allowed a family to bring a malpractice action against their minister alleging that he failed to prevent the suicide of one he was counselling. To avoid such claims, funeral homes sponsoring aftercare activities should undertake the following precautions:

1) Do not refer to grief counselling as therapy or the counselor as a therapist. Terminology such as grief facilitator is recommended.

(2) All funeral home employees that participate in the aftercare program should have grief facilitation training.

(3) The grief facilitator should be trained to refer any serious or apparently serious problems to a psychologist or psychiatrist.

(4) The grief counselling or aftercare program should be covered by the funeral home's malpractice insurance.

5.4   Tort Liability

Funeral directors have to comply with duties and obligations that arise by operation of law as well as those that arise out of the funeral contract. When there is a violation of these duties with resulting damages, a tort has been committed and the court will award damages to those who suffer as a result of the violation of the legal duty.

Two duties recognized by the law which impact directly on the funeral director are: (1) the duty not to interfere with the right of burial; and (2) the duty of exercising reasonable care to keep the funeral home premises or other places under the control of the funeral director in a reasonably safe condition. Violation of these duties that result in damages will make the funeral director liable in tort. The remainder of this section will review those torts that are likely to result from violations of these duties:

a.   Wrongfully Withholding a Body.

The common law generally recognizes that the surviving spouse or the next of kin has the right to the custody of the body, in the condition that it was left in by death, and that such person has the right to dispose of it without interference. The refusal to release the body by a funeral director who has prepared it for burial until he has been paid for his services is widely recognized as an actionable violation of the family's right to burial without interference. For example, in *Morgan v. Richmond*, 336 So.2d 342 (1976), a funeral director who withheld the body of plaintiff's deceased mother until payment was made was liable for damages resulting from the humiliation, embarrassment and mental distress suffered by the plaintiff. A similar result was reached in *Levite Undertakers Co. v. Griggs*, 495 So. 2d 63 (Ala. 1986), where the court found the refusal to release the body "morally reprehensible".

b.   Loss of Body.

There have been cases where the funeral home has misidentified bodies and the funeral home incorrectly interred the wrong one. For example, in *Holsen v. Heritage Mut. Ins. Co.*, 165 Wis. 2d 641, 478 N.W. 2d 59 (1991), the funeral home had mixed-up two bodies and had the plaintiff's father wrongfully interred. When the body was not available for the visitation, the court found that the funeral home had negligently interfered with the family's common law right to properly conduct a funeral.

c.   Mutilation of the Body.

The right of possession of the body for the purpose of burial carries with it the right to receive the body in the condition it was in at the time of death. If the body is mutilated, a tort is committed.

Mutilation, although slight and necessary, is involved in embalming a body. Generally, a funeral director has the right to do this as the mutilation is implicitly sanctioned by the permission given to embalm the body. If, however, the embalming is done without permission, the tort of mutilation of the body occurs.

In *Sworski v. Simons*, 208 Minn. 201, 293 S.W. 309 (1940), a funeral director received an unidentified body from a coroner who advised him to embalm the body. The funeral director followed that advice and embalmed the body before the next of kin could be located. When the next of kin learned of the embalming, he sued the funeral director for mutilation of the body. Because of the embalming had not been authorized by the next of kin, the court permitted the plaintiff to bring the action. The court held that it was not a defense for the funeral director to claim that the embalming was beneficial.

In *Scheuer v. William F. Howard Funeral Home*, 385 S. 2d 1076 (Fla. 1980), the funeral home embalmed without permission and in violation of the decedent's Jewish faith. The funeral director testified that he "was aware the deceased was of the Jewish faith and because of such knowledge saved two bottles of blood to be buried with her." The court permitted the plaintiff to bring an action finding that there was an issue for the jury to decide as to whether the funeral director was aware of the adverse consequences of his decision to immediately embalm the body.

A second, although less likely incidence of mutilation involving funeral directors can occur with unauthorized autopsies. An autopsy is a post-mortem examination of the body, usually for the purposes of determining the cause of death. If the autopsy is not authorized by the next of kin or is not duly ordered by the coroner in the lawful discharge of his duties, it constitutes an actionable tort.

Although funeral directors do not typically conduct the autopsy, they still may be liable if they participate in it or consent to it without the authorization of the next of kin. The court in *Myers v. Clarke*, 122 Ky. 866, 90 S.W. 1049 (1906), held that funeral directors who, without permission of the next of kin, permitted autopsies to be performed will be jointly liable with the person performing the autopsy. Likewise in *Palenske v. Bruning*, 98 Ill. App. 644 (1900), a funeral director who assisted in an unauthorized autopsy was held jointly liable.

However, if the funeral director merely accedes to the demands of the coroner and makes the body available, he will not liable if the subsequent autopsy is not authorized. This was recognized by decision in *Konecny v. Hohenschuh*, 188 Iowa 1075, 173 N.W. 901 (1919) and *Gurganious v. Simpson*, 213 N.C. 613, 197 S.E. 163 (1938). The courts are in an apparent agreement that funeral directors are not required to challenge the coroner's authority to conduct the autopsy in order to avoid possible liability for participating or consenting to an unauthorized autopsy.

d. Injury to Invitees.

A funeral home owes the duty of care to each invitee to the funeral home to maintain the premises in a reasonably safe condition for its intended use. The chapel, staterooms, means of ingress and egress, restrooms and other facilities must be maintained in a reasonably safe condition in order that such invitees in the exercise of ordinary care will not suffer injury.

The degree of the duty of care a landowner owes to a person on the landowner's property depends on the status of the person. A high degree of care is owed to one who has been invited on the property by the land owner; on the other hand, a trespasser is owed a very little degree of care. Persons coming to a funeral home for the purpose of attending funerals, viewing remains, or engaging the funeral director's services have generally been recognized to be "invitees" and therefore, entitled to a high degree of care. Moreover, some courts have heightened that duty of care with funeral homes, reasoning that because invitees to a funeral home are often in an emotionally disturbed state, funeral directors should expect that they will be somewhat less prudent in looking out for themselves than the ordinary man would be.

An example of the above rule was found in *Shipman v. Norton*, 154 Cal. App. 2d 90, 315 P.2d 906 (1957), where the plaintiff injured herself when stepping off a porch onto a step which was made in the same brick pattern material as the porch. The plaintiff claimed the funeral home was negligent in not differentiating the step from the porch. The funeral home defended against the claim by alleging that the plaintiff was contributorily negligent since she had seen the step on her way into the funeral home and should have remembered it on her way out. The court held for the plaintiff finding that if an undifferentiated step was negligent in other contexts, it should be considered even more so in a funeral home situation where it is to be expected that invitees will be emotionally upset after services and not looking out for themselves.

Funeral directors are required by this duty of care to take precaution against snow and ice, especially during services when people will be coming in and out of the funeral home. In both *Watts v. Rhodes*, 325 Mass. 697, 91 N.E.2d 925 (1950) and *Filipiak v. Plombon*, 15 Wis.2d 483, 113 N.W.2d 365 (1962), funeral homes were found liable for injuries resulting from icy walkways and ramps leading to and from the funeral home.

e. Injury to Pallbearers and Clergy.

A funeral director will be liable for an injury suffered to a pallbearer (those who voluntarily carried the casket) or a member of the clergy if the

31

injury is caused by the tort of the funeral director. In *Frederick v. J.E. Hixson and Sons*, 159 So.2d 599 (La. 1964), a minister presiding at graveside service was injured when he slipped on artificial grass mats covering a marble slab. Although the grass mats had been negligently placed on the marble slabs by the vault company, the funeral director was found jointly liable. The court held that the funeral director had full responsibility to control the funeral, which responsibility included the "prior discovery of reasonably discoverable conditions of the premises that may be unreasonably dangerous and correction thereof or a warning to the invitee of the danger". By failing to take proper steps to see that the gravesite was reasonably safe or at least warn those attending the burial services of the hazard, the funeral director breached the duty of care he owed the invitees.

In *Kennedy v. Ricker Funeral Home, Inc.*, 119 N.H. 827, 409 A.2d 778 (1979), the defendant funeral director was held liable for injuries incurred by the plaintiff pallbearer when the pallbearer fell while carrying a handleless casket into the church. An employee of the funeral home asked the plaintiff to help carry the casket into the church and negligently failed to instruct the plaintiff as to how to carry the handleless casket, which by design required the pallbearers to place their fingers in a groove that ran along the sides. While carrying the casket the pallbearer slipped, lost his grip on the casket, and consequently suffered injury to his knee. During the trial there was expert testimony that handleless caskets tend to be unstable and that the defendant had in the past given instructions to people carrying caskets both with and without handles. Thus, the court found that defendant had the duty to instruct the pallbearer in the use of handleless caskets and that he was negligent for failing to do so.

5.5   Mental Anguish

a. Physical Impact.

As a general rule, courts are very reluctant to award damages that cannot be measured with some precision. For this reason, it was traditionally recognized that plaintiffs could not recover monetary damages merely for mental distress or anguish suffered as a result of a contract breach or tort. The courts required some other physical indicia of injury before permitting a plaintiff the right to seek recovery for mental anguish.

The necessity of showing physical injury prior to any recovery for mental anguish is slowly being eroded in American law. This erosion has taken place in many areas. For example, in jurisdictions that still recognized this rule, the requirements has generally been changed from physical injury to physical impact. Thus, it is only necessary to show that there has been some physical impact rather than injury as a threshold to recover damages for mental anguish.

Erosion of the physical impact rule has also occurred in certain areas of the law. No where is this more evident than in actions against funeral directors for contract breaches or torts. Court have taken great pains to create exceptions to the physical impact rule or even to abandon it in order to permit plaintiffs to bring actions against funeral directors. Citing the fact that plaintiffs who have been wronged by funeral directors often have little or no other damages to seek other than damage from mental anguish, courts have devised numerous ways around the physical impact rule.

b. Intentional Infliction of Mental Distress.

As the physical impact rule has been eroded, courts have begun to recognize the tort of intentional infliction of mental distress. This tort permits recovery of damages for mental anguish by the plaintiff when the defendant's conduct is "intentional, wrongful, outrageous, reckless and malicious and done with the intention of causing plaintiff severe emotional distress." *Meyer v. Nottger*, 241 N.W.2d 911 (Iowa 1976).

In explaining this exception, the court in *Estate of Harper v. Orlando Funeral Home, Inc.*, 36 So.2d 126 (Fla. App. 1979), held that absent a physical impact, mental anguish for negligent funeral directing could not be recovered unless plaintiffs allege that defendant's conduct exceeded all bounds reasonably tolerated by society such as to suggest malice or the entire want of care or great indifference. Another Florida court held that such an allegation had been made in *Scherer v. Rubin Memorial Chapel Ltd.*, 444 So.2d 1176 (Fla. App. 1984), wherein the complaint alleged that defendant funeral director had put a body other than decedent's in decedent's casket and burial clothes, that when confronted with this error, defendant tried to convince the plaintiff that the body in question was indeed the decedent, and that after removing the burial clothes from the wrong body, the defendant simply threw the clothes over the decedent's unprepared body. The court ruled that the allegation in the complaint implied sufficient malice to permit recovery for pain, suffering and mental anguish.

c. Contractual Breaches.

Courts in some jurisdictions have relied on the unique nature of funeral contracts to carve out an exception to the physical impact rule. In *Lamm v. Shingleton*, 231 N.C. 10, 55 S.E.2d 810 (1949), the court, noting the personal nature of the funeral contract and the fact that the contract itself puts the funeral director on notice that a breach thereof would probably result in mental anguish, held the damages from mental anguish could be awarded in cases involving breaches of funeral contracts.

The same rationale was applied in *Meyer v. Nottger*, 241 N.W.2d 911 (Iowa 1976), wherein the court permitted recovery for mental anguish as a result of a contractual breach even in the absence of physical trauma because the contract in question was not concerned with trade and commerce, but with life and death and matters of mental concern and solicitude, which should have put the funeral director on notice the mental anguish would result from his breach.

An additional justification for the exception to the physical impact rule was provided for in *Allen v. Jones*, 104 Cal. App. 3d 207, 163 Cal Rptr. 445 (1980). After reciting the fact that the funeral director should be on notice that mental anguish will result from his breach, the court added that the award of damages for mental distress against the funeral director serves as a useful and necessary means to maintain professional standards in the funeral industry. It added that damage for mental anguish is often the only method to compensate victims of wrongful acts by funeral directors.

d. Negligent Infliction of Mental Distress.

As seen earlier, courts now generally recognized that damages for mental anguish can be recovered when the defendant's wrongful conduct is so malicious or reckless that it appears intentionally calculated to cause mental anguish in plaintiffs. Some courts have gone beyond that theory and now permit the recovery of damages for mental anguish in those cases where the wrongful conduct consists merely of simple negligence. In justifying this exception, the courts often use the same rationale as with the funeral contract exception, i.e. funeral directors are on notice that negligent conduct will produce mental anguish and damages for mental anguish are often the only method to compensate victims for such wrongful conduct.

In *Corrigal v. Ball & Dodd Funeral Home, Inc.*, 89 Wash. 2d 959, 577 P.2d 580 (1978), the Washington Supreme Court permitted an action for negligent infliction of mental distress against a funeral director. The court held that proof of simple negligence, as opposed to malicious or reckless conduct, was sufficient to recover damages for mental anguish. A similar result was reached in *Holsen v. Heritage Mut. Ins. Co.*, 165 Wis. 2d 641, 478 N.W. 2d 59 (1991), where the court held that a funeral director could be sued in Wisconsin under the theory of negligent infliction of emotional distress.

Fortunately, those states permitting funeral directors to be sued for negligent infliction of emotional distress are still in the minority. The majority of jurisdictions refuse to permit this action to be brought against funeral directors absent some showing of intentional misconduct or physical impact.

e. Punitive Damages.

Punitive damages are awarded by a court to a plaintiff not to compensate the plaintiff for damages suffered, but to punish the defendant. For this reason, punitive damages are not awarded in cases of simple negligence where the defendant unintentionally caused an injury. They are given only in those cases when the defendant's conduct has been so outrageous as to justify punishment.

These principles have been applied in cases dealing with wrongful conduct of funeral directors. In *Allen v. Jones*, 104 Cal. App.3d 207, 163 Cal. Rptr. 445 (1980), the complaint alleged that the defendant negligently shipped the cremated remains of plaintiff's brother, thereby causing the cremains to be lost. The court dismissed the claim in the complaint for punitive damages, holding that punitive damages could not be recovered in a case involving simple negligence.

In Meyer v. Nottger, 241 N.W.2d 911 (Iowa 1976), however, the court permitted plaintiff to seek punitive damages because they had alleged wrongful conduct that was committed with a wilful and reckless disregard to the rights of others. And in *Golston v. Lincoln Cemetery, Inc.*, 573 S.W.2d 700 (Mo. App. 1978), an award of punitive damages was upheld by an Appellate Court because it found that defendant had shown a complete indifference to or a conscious disregard of the emotional well-being of the plaintiff.

It should be noted that because punitive damages are awarded only in cases of willful or very reckless conduct, it is normally against public policy to insure against this conduct. In other words, most liability insurance policies will not cover awards of punitive damages. Therefore, while funeral director's liability insurance will normally cover damages arising out of the funeral director's negligence, any recovery of punitive damages must be personally paid by the funeral home.

Chapter Six

LIABILITY FOR FUNERAL EXPENSES

6.1 In General

While the care of the family and the proper performance of his duties are the principal concerns of the funeral director, as a responsible businessman he also has an obligation to the funeral home. In order to maintain the economic survival of that enterprise, he must be able to collect funeral bills in a timely manner. It is therefore his responsibility to ascertain who will pay for the funeral and to ensure that person is legally bound to make that payment.

The funeral home has a number of potential sources to look to for the payment of the funeral bill: the estate of the decedent, the surviving spouse, a parent (if the decedent is a minor), any person who signs the contract with the funeral home, or, in the last resort, the government. As seen in this chapter, the legal liability of these various parties will depend on a number of factors. The prudent funeral director will ensure that a solvent party has a legal obligation to pay for the funeral before he agrees to render such services.

6.2 Liability of the Estate

a. Primary Obligor.

When a person dies, the real and personal property owned by him at the time of his death constitutes his "estate". Real property is land and anything attached to it; personal property is any tangible or intangible property such as personal effects, furniture, automobiles, jewelry, money, stocks, bonds, insurance proceeds payable to the estate, and the like.

As a rule, the estate is primarily responsible to pay the reasonable and necessary expenses of disposing of the body. If the estate has property, the funeral director may look to it for payment of the funeral bill. The funeral bill is not a debt of the decedent but is a charge against the estate and must, at least in part, be paid before any debts left by the decedent are met. The amount of the funeral bill which receives this preferential treatment depends upon state law.

The laws of many states limit the amount of a funeral bill which is given the status as a preferential claim against the estate. For example, in Ohio, the funeral director has a preferred claim against the estate for up to $3,000.00. This does not mean that funeral bills in Ohio cannot exceed $3,000.00. It does mean, however, that if a funeral bill is charged to the estate, it receives

37

preferential treatment over other claims against the estate up to the amount of $3,000.00. Any amount in excess of $3,000.00 still is an allowable claim against the estate, although it is not a preferential claim.

b. Reasonableness of the Funeral Bill.

If the decedent leaves a will that authorizes payment of funeral expenses, such provision is enforceable against the estate if it has sufficient assets to pay the bill. If the decedent does not leave a will, or if the will does not specifically provide for the payment of funeral expenses, the amount of funeral expenses properly charged against the estate will, in the absence of a statutory provision, be limited by the probate court to a reasonable amount.

If the court finds that the funeral bill is unreasonably high, it will not permit assets of the estate to be used to pay that amount which it finds to be unreasonable. In determining the reasonableness of a funeral bill, the courts will look at the following factors: (1) the size and solvency of the estate; (2) the right of the creditors; (3) the station in life of the decedent; (4) the decedent's religious faith; (5) the decedent's fraternal memberships; (6) local and contemporary custom; and (7) the funeral director's knowledge of the financial condition of the decedent.

The reasonableness of the funeral bill is often measured in relation to the size of the estate. For example, in *Succession of Smith*, 330 So.2d 402 (La.App. 1976), the court held that funeral charges amounting to $4,599 charged against an estate worth $26,500, although bordering on the excessive, were not out of proportion with the value of the estate.

The court must also weigh the station in life to which the decedent belonged. If the decedent maintained a higher position in life, a more expensive funeral may be justified. Likewise, if the local, ethical or religious customs to which the decedent adhered to require a more elaborate funeral, the court will be more inclined to permit a more expensive bill. Finally, the court may look at the knowledge of the funeral director. If the funeral director contracts for a pretentious funeral although he knows the estate is modest, the court will be less willing to permit the estate to pay the expensive funeral bill. On the other hand, if the funeral director had no knowledge that the estate was small, a court will be more inclined to approve a higher funeral bill.

c. Collection Against an Estate.

One of the principal disadvantages of looking to the estate for payment of the funeral bill is the delay in collection. Probate of an estate can often take up to a year or two after the death of the decedent. While probate laws in most states permit executors to pay funeral expenses from the estate even before the executor is appointed by the court, funeral directors in many cases encounter problems in promptly collecting funeral bills from estates. For these

38

reasons, it is advisable for funeral directors to have additional parties execute the funeral contract. This enables the funeral director to collect the funeral bill from third parties if the estate delays in the payment of the bill.

6.3 Liability for Funeral Expenses of Dependent

The common law rule is that a husband and father are primarily liable to pay the funeral expenses of the wife and dependent children. This is true regardless of whether the wife or child leaves an estate or whether the husband or father sign the funeral contract. Moreover, the husband or father cannot recoup the funeral expenses from the decedent's estate. In other words, the husband or father is primarily liable and the estate is secondarily liable for the funeral expenses.

Because the common law rule has been superseded in some states by statutes making the estate primarily liable for funeral expenses, it is necessary for each funeral director to be aware of his or her own state laws. In addition, if the wife or child specifically provides in her or his will that the estate is to pay for the funeral, the husband or father's duty to pay the expenses are superseded by the estate. Finally, it should be noted that if another member of the family or a third party executes the funeral contract and agrees to become primarily liable to pay for it, the husband or father's obligation is extinguished.

Under the common law, the duty of the husband is not affected by the fact that the husband and wife are separated at the time of her death. Nor is his liability avoided by the fact that he did not arrange the funeral, that he did not attend it, or even that he was not aware of her death.

In general, under the common law there is no duty on the wife to pay for her husband's funeral. However, in some jurisdictions an exception to this rule is recognized where the husband's estate is inadequate to pay for the expenses. In addition, in some states there are statutes making a wife equally chargeable for family expenses thereby abrogating the common law and making her responsible for the husband's funeral expenses.

For example, in *Davis-Turner Funeral Home, Inc. v. Chaney*, 61 O.Misc.2d 76 (1991), a widow, who refused to pay for her husband's funeral, was compelled to reimburse her stepson who paid for the funeral. The court held that under Ohio law a wife is statutorily obligated to pay for the funeral expenses of her husband when the estate is insolvent.

6.4 Contractual Liability

The person who requests a funeral director to undertake a funeral does not automatically make himself liable for the funeral expenses. Unless the law implies liability on his part because of his legal relation to the decedent or because he expressly or implicitly agrees to become individually liable for the funeral expense, he will not be responsible for the funeral bill. In some jurisdictions, a widow will become personally liable for the funeral expenses merely by the fact that she requests or orders the funeral arrangements. Cases from these jurisdictions hold that in the absence of a special understanding that the funeral home is to look only to the estate for payment, the widow who arranges the funeral will be liable. Of course, this rule does not apply in those states wherein the statutory law makes the estate primarily liable.

Although an unrelated third party is not liable for funeral expenses even if he arranges the funeral, he can agree by oral or written contract to make himself personally liable to pay the funeral expenses. If a third party or a relative agrees to become personally liable on the contract, the funeral director should have the party execute a written contract. Moreover, in those cases where there is a question about the size or solvency of the estate, it is prudent for the funeral director to have a relative or third party become liable on the contract in the event the estate is unable to pay the funeral expenses.

6.5   Liability of Executor or Administrator

Usually the executor or administrator of the decedent's estate is not appointed until the funeral director has been summoned and the funeral completed. Therefore, the question of his liability seldom arises. In those cases where the executor or administrator engages the service of the funeral director for the decedent, he may be personally bound to pay the funeral expenses unless he has stipulated against personal liability, or the circumstances are such as to clearly show that the funeral director was looking to the estate for primary payment. If an executor or administrator pays for the funeral from his own funds, he may be reimbursed by the estate for the reasonable expense of the funeral.

In *Davis-Turner Funeral Home, Inc. v. Chaney*, supra, the son had been appointed as executor for his father's estate. However, in signing the funeral contract, he had not stipulated that he was signing as the executor of the estate. Therefore, he was personally responsible for paying the bill. Fortunately for the son, the court found that the funeral expenses were ultimately the responsibility of the surviving spouse and ordered her to reimburse the son for those expenses.

Where an executor is vested by a will with authority to expend for funeral expenses such amount as he deems proper, the exercise of his discretion will not be reviewed by the probate court in the absence of a showing that he arbitrarily and improperly determined the amount to be expended for funeral expenses.

6.6   Liability of State

Where a funeral is ordered by a public official in the performance of the duties of his office, the state or one of its subdivisions may be rendered liable to the funeral director for the funeral. Of course, before agreeing to perform such a funeral, the funeral director should ensure that the state or one of its subdivisions will accept responsibility for payment of the bill.

State and local governments may also be responsible by law for the full or partial payment of indigent funerals. Funeral directors need to know what government agencies make funds available for indigent funerals and how to make claims for those funds.

Chapter Seven

CREMATION

7.1   Overview

The level of cremation in the United States has continued at a steady growth rate for the past twenty years. The cremation rate in the U.S. is currently 20% and experts predict that the rate will increase to 25% by the year 2000. Factors which have led to the increase include a growing acceptance by the public of cremation, the relocation of the elderly to Florida, Arizona, and other areas in the sunbelt, the influx of immigrants from cultures that prefer cremation, and a higher level of education in the American public.

In response to this trend, many funeral directors are expanding the goods and services they offer to families that desire cremation. Innovative funeral directors understand that cremation can often be part of a meaningful funeral experience. Cremation opens up new options and services for the family and the funeral director.

As well as increasing options, cremation also greatly increases the potential legal liability of funeral directors. Because cremation is an irreversible process, mistakes made by funeral directors often cannot be undone. This irreparable nature of cremation is the underlying reason why funeral directors must be extremely cautious in conducting business in this area.

In recent years, a rash of cremation liability lawsuits, especially from California, has alerted the funeral industry to the necessity of precautions in arranging and handling cremation. The remainder of this chapter looks at areas of potential liability and precautions that funeral directors should adopt.

7.2   Authorization to Cremate

a. Identification.

Certainly one of the most serious civil misdeeds that a funeral home can commit is the cremation of the wrong body. Because cremation is irreversible, there is no way to remedy the wrongdoing. Moreover, for a family who desires burial, the emotional damage of being deprived of the body for burial can often be devastating. The funeral home that mistakenly cremates a body that was to have another type of disposition will undoubtedly be the subject of a lawsuit seeking a substantial monetary recovery.

To avoid any possibility of cremating the wrong body, funeral directors should insist upon a positive identification of the body by the spouse or next of kin. The body should be viewed by the spouse or next of kin and a written representation by them attesting to the identity of the deceased should be obtained and placed in a permanent file. In addition, the funeral home should have established safeguards throughout the handling of the body to insure that the body is never misidentified.

  b. *Written Authorization.*

  To protect the funeral home from liability, it is imperative that the funeral director obtain written authorization to cremate the body. The authorization should be signed by that person who has the primary right of disposition, e.g. the surviving spouse and/or the next of kin. In cases where there are several people holding the primary right of disposition, the prudent funeral director will want to receive written authorization from each of them. If one of them cannot be located after diligent efforts to do so, the individuals authorizing the cremation should indicate in writing that they do not know of any objection to the cremation by the individual who could not be contacted. Additionally, the funeral director will want those authorizing the cremation to indemnify the funeral home if the individual not authorizing the cremation later brings suit.

  In cases where the next of kin is at a distant location, the funeral director may obtain signed written authorization by fax. Most individuals have access to a fax machine and can send a signed authorization giving their consent to the cremation. The faxed authorization will serve as evidence that the funeral director has received consent to cremate the body.

  c. *Informed Consent.*

  One of the claims made in recent cases on cremation liability is that the surviving spouse or next of kin did not give "informed" consent. In those cases, the plaintiff admits giving permission to cremate, but alleges that such consent was invalid because the consumer did not fully understand the cremation process.

  Because the potential liability in this area is so great, most experts now recommend that cremation consent forms signed by the surviving spouse or next of kin contain a detailed explanation of the cremation process. By informing the consumer exactly how the cremation is carried out, how cremains are gathered and processed, and what cremains the consumer will receive after the cremation, the funeral director can avoid claims by the family that its consent was invalid because it did not fully understand the process.

7.3   Wrongdoing in the Cremation Process

  It is clear that funeral directors who operate a crematory will be responsible for any wrongdoing or omission at the crematory. However, even for those funeral directors not operating a crematory, liability for crematory wrongdoings may be imputed to the funeral home. Because the funeral home often contracts with the crematory and because of the funeral director's over-all supervisory responsibility in caring for the body, some courts have al-lowed families to sue funeral directors for the misdeeds of independent cre-matories.

In view of this liability, all funeral directors operating a crematory or doing business with an independent crematory must be cognizant of any of the following wrongdoings or omissions:

a. *Commingling of Remains.*

One of the unethical practices that was the subject of many of the cremation liability cases in California was the commingling of remains. Cre-matory operators, in order to save costs, were cremating multiple bodies at the same time and commingling cremains. As a result, survivors were not sure whether the urn they received contained their relative's cremains, cremains from a stranger, or some mixture of both.

To protect against liability in this area, crematory operators must al-ways insure that only one body is cremated at a time. (Occasionally, with a multiple death from a family, the survivors may request that two bodies be cremated simultaneously. Obviously, in this case, authorization for the com-mingling should be in writing.) Likewise, funeral directors dealing with inde-pendent crematories should insure that the crematory has a strict policy against multiple cremations without written consent.

Because it is impossible to remove all the cremains from a retort each time, some small amount of commingling is inevitable. For this reason, the written authorization to cremate should explain that some commingling will result. This is part of the "informed" consent that the surviving spouse or next of kin should understand and agree to in writing prior to the cremation.

b. *Failure to Remove All Cremains.*

There have been cremation liability cases where the family alleges that the crematory did not return all of the cremains. In some of these cases, the urn was not sufficient to hold all the cremains and the excess cremains were discarded by unethical or careless crematory operators. These opera-tors were found liable for damages.

If a funeral director or crematory operator is faced with a situation where the urn is insufficient to hold all the cremains, the excess cremains should be placed in a temporary plastic urn and returned to the family. When selling urns, funeral directors should inform the family that certain urns may not be sufficient to hold the cremains. The written authorization form should also alert the family that any excess cremains not fitting into the urn will be placed in a temporary urn and returned to them. Finally, the cremation authorization form should also warn the family that it is impossible to recover all the cremains from the retort and that some may be lost in the process.

c. Jewelry and Medical Devices.

One area a funeral director must address with the family requesting embalming is the removal and disposal of jewelry and medical devices. Since jewelry is destroyed in the cremation process, the family should specify in writing what jewelry, if any, is to remain on the body.

The issue of medical devices is one of liability to the crematory operators. Some medical devices, such as pacemakers, can explode in a retort causing damage. There is also potential danger if radioactive implants are cremated. Funeral directors should inquire from the family whether the decedent had any implanted medical devices or prostheses. If they do, the funeral director should obtain written permission to remove the devices prior to cremation and instructions as to disposal of such devices.

7.4   Misdelivery of Cremains

If a funeral director receives cremains back from the crematory, he will be responsible for the proper handling and delivery of those cremains to the spouse or next of kin. In the event that the cremains are lost or improperly commingled with other cremains, the funeral director will be liable. For example, in *Allen v. Jones*, 104 Cal. App. 3d 207, 163 Cal. Rptr. 445 (1980), a funeral home that negligently packed the cremains in a shipping carton thereby causing the package to be lost was liable for breach of contract.

In *Corrigal v. Ball & Dodd Funeral Home, Inc.*, 89 Wash. 2d 959, 577 P. 2d 580 (1978), a mother received a package containing the cremains of her son. The funeral director had not placed the cremains in the urn as agreed to nor had he advised the mother that the urn was not in the package. The mother, believing she was sifting through packing material looking for the urn, was actually running her hands through the cremains. When she sued the funeral home for its failure to place the cremains in the urn as contracted for, the court held that she had stated a cause of action for negligent infliction of mental distress.

Given the abundance of litigation concerning the misdelivery of cremains, funeral directors should undertake the following precautions:

a. Written Instructions.

It is imperative that funeral directors obtain detailed written instructions in the cremation authorization form as to where and how the cremains are to be returned to the family or otherwise disposed. If the family wishes to pick up the cremains directly from the funeral home, the written authorization should designate the individual or individuals to whom the funeral home is authorized to release the cremains. Obviously, funeral homes should never turn over cremains to one not specifically authorized to receive them. To protect themselves, funeral directors should request the individual receiving the cremains to sign a receipt.

    b. Shipping of Cremains.

If the family desires the funeral director to arrange shipping of the cremains, the family should designate in writing on the cremation authorization the shipper and the method of shipment. For example, if the shipment is to be by overnight courier, the family should list on the authorization form which delivery company is to be utilized. The cremains should be securely packed in a temporary plastic urn with a triple container. It is also strongly recommended that the authorization form contain a release of liability of the funeral director for any loss of the cremains during shipment.

    c. Storage.

There are many funeral homes in the country that are storing cremains because family members fail to take delivery of them. These funeral directors, some who may be holding cremains for as long as twenty years, are fearful of disposing of the cremains because of liability. However, since the family refuses to pick up their remains or is no longer able to be contacted, the funeral home has been converted into an unwilling warehouse for stored cremains.

To avoid this problem, it is recommended that the cremation authorization form state that a storage charge will be imposed after a certain period. Oftentimes, these storage fees will encourage the family to retrieve the cremains. It is also advisable to include in the authorization permission for the funeral home to dispose of the cremains "in any lawful manner" if the cremains are not picked up after a certain length of time. While any "lawful manner" may include scattering the cremains, this method of disposal is not recommended since it would be impossible to retrieve the cremains at a later date. Rather, out of an abundance of caution, the funeral director may want to purchase a lot at a cemetery and inter all unclaimed cremains in a vault that would allow the family to recover the cremains at a later date.

Chapter Eight

DISINTERMENT

8.1   Disinterment Defined

Disinterment, or exhumation as it is sometimes called, may be defined as the removal of a dead body or remains from its place of repose after disposition has been completed. In the case of a burial, it means digging up and removal of the remains; in the case of cremation, the removal of ashes from their repository.

8.2   Disinterment Disfavored

In most jurisdictions, there is a strong public policy against disinterment. Many judicial decisions indicate that disinterment is not a matter of right and that ordinarily a court will not order or permit a body to be disinterred unless there is a strong showing that it is necessary and that the interest of justice requires the disinterment. Even the individual with the paramount right of disposition cannot disinter the body against the will of other relatives except upon strong and convincing evidence that persuades a court of equity that the disinterment is required by justice.

Many of the cases indicate that the law in principle abhors disinterment out of respect for the human desire not to have one's remains disturbed, the sentiment of survivors and the protection of public health. Therefore, disinterment is allowable only in cases where good cause for it is shown by the parties seeking to disinter a body.

Disinterment may be authorized by law on two principal grounds, either in the public interest or for private purposes. In the former, the public purpose may be to further some matter of public interest although the immediate reason may be private. In the latter, the purpose is purely private.

8.3   Disinterment in the Public Interest

Exhumations in the public interest usually involve the disinterment of the body and its reinterment in the same place. In such cases, the exhumation is normally made for evidentiary purposes, either for criminal or civil cases.

It is well-established that the state has the power to seek an exhumation for the purposes of gathering evidence for a criminal trial. Courts will readily grant enforcement officers the authority to exhume bodies if required for criminal investigations or trials.

In some cases, a party may seek to affirm or disaffirm an alleged cause of death in connection with an insurance policy. In these cases, exhumation for evidentiary purposes is permitted on the grounds that the possible existence of fraud should not be protected by the rule forbidding the disturbance of the repose of the dead. However, in civil cases such as these, a stronger burden of proof is usually required by the parties seeking disinterment than is required in criminal cases. For example, in *Application of Coleman*, 153 NYS 2d 936, a court denied the request of the decedent's sister to have the decedent's body disinterred for purposes of examination to ascertain the cause of death. Although the sister suspected foul play, the court noted that there had been an autopsy prior to burial, that the sister's suspicions were based on hearsay and on statements not under oath, and that there was nothing in the sister's application to indicate that public officials had failed to properly determine the cause of death.

Disinterment of a body and its reinterment in a different place may be made in the public interest to provide access for public streets. Bodies have also been disinterred in the public interest where they may constitute a threat to public health, such as the possibility of contaminating well water.

8.4   Disinterment for Private Purposes

Exhumation for private purposes generally involves disinterment and reinterment at another place. There can be many reasons for private parties to seek disinterment. For example, the surviving spouse or next of kin may be dissatisfied with the place of interment. Oftentimes, due to the relocation of the family and a desire to be close to the place of interment, a family may seek to move the body to a cemetery within their locale. Bodies have sometimes been mistakenly interred in cemetery lots not owned by the family. In other cases, cemeteries have been abandoned or in such disrepair that the court will allow disinterment.

In many states, disinterment is a matter of statutory regulation. The usual procedure requires the surviving spouse and/or next of kin to make a written application to the trustees of the cemetery. A funeral director may be required to be in attendance during the disinterment. Restrictions may be placed upon disinterment by the state for public health reasons.

Where no statutes govern the procedure, case law is controlling. Any interested party may make an application to a court of equity which then determines whether to grant the application for disinterment. Generally, the surviving spouse and/or the next of kin have the primary right to seek disinterment.

In determining whether there is good cause to order a disinterment, courts have indicated that each case must turn on its own particular facts.

Nevertheless, when deciding whether reasonable cause exists for disinterment, courts have looked at the following factors: (1) the degree of the relationship that the party seeking disinterment bears to the decedent; (2) the degree of the relationship that the party seeking to prevent disinterment bears to the decedent; (3) the express wishes of the decedent; (4) the conduct of persons seeking disinterment, especially as it may relate to circumstances of the original interment; (5) the conduct of persons seeking to prevent disinterment; (6) the length of time that has elapsed since the original interment; (7) the strength of reasons offered both in favor and opposition to disinterment; (8) the integrity and compassion of persons seeking disinterment to provide a secure and comparable resting place for the decedent; and (9) the rights and principles of the religious body or other institution which granted the right to inter the body at the first place of burial.

Often a court will have to balance competing interests and make a choice based upon the judge's determination as to the importance of each factor. For example, in *Guerin v. Cassidy*, 38 N.J. 454, 119 A.2d 780 (1955), the decedent, a Catholic, was buried in a Catholic cemetery. Later when her will was discovered, the executor petitioned the court to allow removal to another Catholic cemetery which decedent had named in her will. After balancing factors involved in the case, the court refused permission to disinter, finding as follows:

> "Although it may be recognized that the wishes or directions of the deceased as to his interment are entitled to respectful consideration and are allowed great weight, such directions, even though contained in a will, are not considered testamentary in nature, since there is no property right in a dead body in the ordinary sense. After interment, a body is in the custody of the law and removal is subject to the jurisdiction of this court. Such power, however, should not be exercised unless it is clearly shown that good cause and urgent necessity for such action exists. In light of the fact that the decedent is already buried in ground which, according to ecclesiastical law and the doctrine of her church, is consecrated and hallowed, and the cost incident to the removal to another cemetery would be excessive when compared to the size of the estate, there appears to be no good cause or urgent necessity to direct such removal."

Although religious law may be evidence to show the customs and wishes of those who observe its mandates, it is not binding on the court. In *Tamarkin v. Children of Israel, Inc.*, 2 O. App. 2d 60 (1965) the defendant, an Orthodox

Jewish cemetery, sought to prevent the decedent's next of kin from removing the decedent's remains to a Reformed Jewish Cemetery. The court held that the restriction in the cemetery deed prohibiting removal was in conflict with the statutory right of the next of kin to seek disinterment. The court therefore permitted the removal on the basis that a private contract grounded in ecclesiastical law cannot nullify an existing statute.

Oftentimes courts are called upon to settle family disputes regarding disinterment. In *Mallen v. Mallen*, 520 S.W. 2d 736 (Tenn. 1974), a widow sought to have her husband's remains removed from her in-laws' property. The evidence showed that the parents of the decedent and the wife were very hostile to each other.

The court stated that there were a number of factors involved in the decision. First, the court noted that the parties were Jewish and that Jewish custom did not favor disinterment. The court also recognized the judicial principle that courts do not ordinarily permit disinterment unless there is a compelling reason to justify it.

However, the court noted that in this case there was no record of what the preferences of the decedent were. When there has been no request or express wish on the part of the decedent and there arises a conflict among the spouse and blood relations, the court found that the wishes of the spouse should command first consideration. In that respect, the court ruled as follows:

> "In past cases, many justifications have permitted disinterment by a surviving spouse. A few which might be mentioned are the fulfillment of the surviving spouse's expectation, where it was understood that the original interment was to only be temporary; the obtainment of side-by-side burial plots; reinterment in a location more accessible to the spouse; and reinterment in a location removed from family hostility."

Balancing the factors, the court allowed the wife to disinter the body and relocate it to another cemetery.

It is apparent that there are many diverse reasons for seeking disinterment and that it is impossible to judge the validity of them in advance of a decision by the court. Like many other situations encountered in the field of mortuary law, these cases each stand upon their own merits. If a funeral director has any doubts as to the proper authorization for disinterment, he should not participate in such disinterment until he has been assured that it has been legally authorized.

8.5 Unauthorized Disinterments

It is an indictable offense under statute and common law to disinter a dead body without proper authority regardless of the purpose or motive. It was held in the case of *State of North Carolina v. McLean*, 121 N.C. 589 (1897), that the members of a Board of Commissioners, who opened graves in a town cemetery for the purpose of removing bodies for reburial in the free section of the cemetery because the original graves were unpaid for, were guilty of a statute forbidding disinterment except with the consent of a surviving spouse or next of kin.

Chapter Nine

FUNERAL HOMES

9.1   Defined

A funeral home is a fixed place for the conducting of funerals and/or for the care and preparation of the dead prior to disposition. The determination of whether an establishment constitutes a funeral home will depend upon the activities carried on at that place. Generally, if dead bodies are taken to the establishment for preparation prior to burial or other disposition, or if funerals are conducted at the establishment (other than a religious establishment), the building will be considered a funeral home.

9.2   Licensing and Regulation

Just as the police power of state and local governments authorizes the licensing and regulation of funeral directors, it also permits the licensing and regulation of funeral homes. In most states there are comprehensive laws and administrative regulations governing the operation of funeral homes. Funeral homes are subject to inspection by government agencies to insure hygiene, health and safety. Moreover, as seen in Chapter Thirteen, funeral homes are increasingly under the scrutiny of the Occupational Safety and Health Administration, the federal agency responsible for safe working conditions.

With regard to licensing, courts have routinely upheld restrictions that state governments have placed on who may operate a funeral home. For example, a Pennsylvania law allowing professional or restricted corporations to establish branch funeral homes, but denying business corporations that privilege was upheld in *H.B. Brandt Funeral Home, Inc. v. Commonwealth*, 78 Pa. Cmwlth. 206, 467 A.2d 106 (1983). The court ruled that the law served a legitimate state goal of protecting the public. The court reasoned that since professional and restricted corporations were owned by licensed funeral directors and their families, the legislature could reasonably assume that these operations would conduct their businesses in accordance with the highest standards of the funeral profession. However, since business corporations could be owned by non-licensed shareholders, the profit motives of the shareholders could influence the funeral home's operation so that it was not conducted in accordance with the standards of funeral homes owned by professional or restricted corporations.

While courts will routinely uphold laws restricting funeral home operations that have any rational relationship to public health or safety, courts tend to examine administrative regulations of state boards with greater scrutiny. For example, in *Labach v. Board of Embalmers and Funeral Directors*, 12 N.J. Super 334, 79 A.2d 693 (1951), the court rejected a rule of the State Board that prohibited a funeral director from serving as a manager of more than one funeral home. The court held that the regulation did not have any reasonable relationship to the safeguarding of the public health. Similarly, in *Golubski v. Board of Embalmers*, 114 O. App. 111, 180 N.E.2d 861 (1961), the court found that the State Board could not prohibit the serving of food or intoxicating liquor in conjunction with a funeral since such powers exceeded the Board's statutory authority.

9.3 Location of Funeral Homes

a. Nuisance.

Under the common law, a nuisance is an invasion of a landowner's interest in the reasonable use and enjoyment of his land. Put differently, a nuisance is an unreasonable, unusual, or unnatural use of one's property so that it disturbs the peaceful, quiet and undisturbed use and enjoyment of nearby property.

In communities where the location of funeral homes is not governed by zoning laws or other regulation, funeral homes have sometimes been the target of nuisance actions brought by adjoining landowners. Typically, these suits have alleged that the presence of the funeral home causes psychological depression to neighbors as well as a depreciation in property values.

Recognizing that funeral homes are lawful and necessary businesses for the public health and safety, courts have generally refused to declare that funeral homes are nuisances. However, in some cases where funeral homes are located in an area that is strictly or predominantly residential in nature, funeral homes have been found to be a nuisance. For example, in *Higgins v. Bloch*, 213 Ala. 209, 104 So. 429 (1925), the court held that the proposed establishment of a funeral home in a long-standing residential neighborhood would constitute a nuisance in that it would depreciate property values and inconvenience, disturb and depress neighboring homeowners.

Nuisance suits have not faired well when the funeral home is located in a business area or an area in transition. In *Potter v. Bryan Funeral Home*, 307 Ark. 142, 817 S.W. 2d 882 (1991), property owners sought to stop a funeral home by arguing that it would depress property values. The court dismissed this suit noting that there were four or five other businesses within

56

two blocks of the proposed funeral home. Therefore, when the area in question is a mix of commercial and residential uses, nuisance suits generally will not prevail.

b. *Zoning Regulations.*

As part of its police power, municipalities have the general authority to adopt zoning ordinances. A zoning ordinance is a regulation dividing the municipality into geographical sections and specifying for each such section the nature, character and use of buildings or occupancy within that section. For example, the zoning plan may designate a certain area as "residential", thereby precluding the establishment of business enterprises in that particular area.

Although many older funeral home buildings in this country may have at one time served as a residence, it is well-recognized that a funeral home is a commercial use or business use of property, and not a residential use. It, therefore, follows that a funeral home may not be established in a residential area since it constitutes a business. On the other hand, since funeral homes are a legitimate business use of property, they may be established in most areas zoned for commercial use. This offers the funeral home protection against objecting neighbors. For example, when neighbors challenged a funeral home as a nuisance in *Linsler v. Booth Undertaking Company*, 120 Wash. 177, 206 P. 676 (1922), the court dismissed the suit noting that the funeral home was located in a district zoned for business use. The zoning ordinance shielded the funeral home from the nuisance claim.

While funeral homes generally cannot be operated in an area zoned for residential use, there are certain exceptions. If a municipality adopts a new zoning ordinance or changes an existing ordinance, it will often "grandfather" existing non-conforming uses. For example, if a funeral home was already operating in an area that a new zoning ordinance designates as residential, the law may permit the property to be maintained as a funeral home even though it does not conform to the new zoning use. While this allows the funeral home to continue, it may restrict any expansion, renovation or rebuilding of the current structure. Moreover, once the funeral home operation ceases in that building, it can no longer be used as a funeral home.

When establishing residential areas by zoning regulations, a municipality may permit professional offices to be operated out of a residence. In cases where a doctor, dentist, musician or other professional lives in the residence, he or she has been permitted to operate an office out of the house. Most jurisdictions that permit such office use by professionals have ruled that funeral directing is not a profession that qualifies for this exception. The prevailing view by courts is that the occupation of a funeral director is a business and not a profession.

Residential zoning ordinances have also occasionally permitted places of assembly or public or quasi-public buildings to be maintained in a residential area. Generally, these exceptions are enacted to permit theaters or other places of amusement in neighborhoods. Most courts have ruled that funeral homes do not qualify as either a place of assembly or a public building, and therefore, this exception is not available to funeral homes.

c. Conclusion.

It is generally very difficult to establish a new funeral home in a residential area. Because of restrictive zoning laws or the possibility of a nuisance suit, most funeral homes are now located in strictly commercial areas or areas that permit joint use by businesses and residences. Of course, because of grandfathering provisions in zoning ordinances, there are still many funeral homes operating in predominantly residential areas across the country.

Obviously, a funeral director planning to build a funeral home or to convert an existing building into a funeral home must carefully research existing zoning laws in the municipality to determine if such property use is permissible. If no zoning ordinances are in place, an evaluation of the area should be made to ascertain if neighboring landowners will object to the funeral home. The assistance of a real estate attorney with expertise in zoning matters is usually recommended.

9.4 Americans With Disabilities Act

a. Overview.

One of the principal purposes of the Americans With Disabilities Act (ADA) is to provide disabled individuals with full use and enjoyment of public accommodations. The public accommodation related section of the ADA took effect on January 26, 1992. Generally, it requires businesses to remove architectural, communication and transportation barriers, provided that such removal is "readily achievable", i.e. the removal can be accomplished without much difficulty or expense taking into consideration the cost of the removal as well as the size and financial resources of the business.

Since funeral homes are defined as public accommodations, they are subject to this section of the ADA. The ADA has two sets of standards for public accommodations. The more stringent standards are for those buildings or additions that were first occupied after January, 1993. Since the law was enacted in July, 1990, any new building that was constructed for occupancy after January, 1993 should have been designed to fully comply with the ADA stringent standards.

For older buildings that existed prior to January, 1993, the ADA prescribes a more relaxed standard. However, as seen below, this standard may require funeral homes to make substantial investments in order to be in compliance with the ADA.

b. *Priorities.*

In undertaking the process of removing barriers to disabled individuals, the ADA sets out a priority list for owners of public accommodations. The first priority is for the owner to provide access to the facility from public sidewalks, parking facilities and public transportations. Therefore, the owner's first priority should be to erect permanent ramps, widen entrance doorways, make curb cuts and designate disabled parking areas.

The second priority for the building owner is to provide access to areas of the public accommodation where goods or services are made available to the public. For example, the funeral director should insure access to chapels and visitation areas, arrangement offices and casket sales areas. Assistive listening devices should be installed in chapels. Furniture should be rearranged to permit sufficient space in aisles for access by wheelchairs, and shelves and other displays should be repositioned so that sale items can be displayed to those who are not standing.

The third priority is to establish access to restroom facilities. Doors and toilet stall areas should be widened, toilet seats raised, grab bars installed, paper towel dispensers lowered and full length mirrors installed.

The final priority is to take any other measures needed to insure access to goods, services and the facilities of the public accommodation. This would include repositioning public telephones, lowering drinking fountains, removing any high pile carpet which impedes access by wheelchair bound individuals, adding raised markings on elevator control buttons for sight impaired individuals, installing flashing alarm lights for hearing impaired individuals, and installing accessible door hardware.

c. *Readily Achievable Test.*

Some of the barrier removals cited above can involve significant expense to the owner of the funeral home. It is important to note that all barrier removals are not necessarily required by the ADA. The ADA requires only those removables which are "readily achievable".

In determining if removal is readily achievable, the ADA directs the owner of the public accommodation to evaluate the following factors:

(1) the cost and nature of the removal;

(2) the overall financial resources of the business, the number of people employed at the site, the expense of instituting the removal, and the impact it will have on the operation of the business; and

(3) if there is a parent company, the overall resources of the parent. For example, a barrier removal that is not readily achievable for an independent funeral home may be readily achievable by a firm that is part of a large conglomerate.

In the first analysis, the owner of the public accommodation is the judge of what is readily achievable. The regulations promulgated under the ADA indicate that each case will be judged on its particular facts and weight will be accorded to the business judgment of the owner. However, if an owner's decision not to remove a barrier is challenged, the owner has the burden of proof in showing that the removal was not readily achievable.

If challenged, two factors will help the owner's defense. First, if the owner can show that the business engaged in a self assessment and made a deliberate decision not to remove a barrier, it will show a good faith effort with compliance. The second factor which assists the owner's defense is to show that the owner instituted, or at least investigated, alternatives to the barrier removal. For example, if a funeral home has its casket display room on a second floor which is not accessible to wheelchair bound individuals, it would show good faith if the funeral home had assembled a binder containing photographs and detailed descriptions of all its casket offerings for those individuals who did not have access to the casket display room.

d. *Withholding of Services.*

The ADA protects not only disabled individuals but also anyone with a close relationship to the disabled individual. Therefore, family members of disabled individuals generally are within the protective scope of the ADA.

If an individual with AIDS or other contagious disease dies, a funeral home that refuses to embalm the body or offer funeral services has violated the ADA. The family members of that deceased disabled individual may bring an action under the ADA against the funeral home.

It is also important to note that in offering services to disabled individuals and their families, owners of public accommodations cannot impose surcharges for extra costs that may be imposed. In the case of funeral directors, contagious disease surcharges for embalming are prohibited by the ADA. Individual lawsuits and enforcement actions by the Department of Justice have been brought against funeral homes that impose surcharges when embalming individuals that have died of contagious disease.

e. Enforcement.

The public accommodations section of the ADA may be enforced by either the U.S. Attorney General's office or private individuals. If a public accommodation is found to have violated the ADA, the court may order the business to remove a barrier and fine the business up to $50,000 for a first offense and $100,000 for subsequent violations. In addition, the court may award attorneys' fees to a private plaintiff.

Chapter Ten

PRENEED FUNERAL CONTRACTS

10.1 In General

Preneed funeral contracts refer to contracts entered into between members of the public and funeral directors to provide for funeral goods and services in the future upon the death of the contract beneficiary. The purchaser of the preneed contract typically prefunds the contract either through a payment made to the funeral director at the time the contract is entered into or by the purchase of an insurance policy upon the life of the contract beneficiary. When the contract beneficiary dies, the funeral director carries out the terms of the contract and provides the promised funeral goods and services.

Preneed contracts may be guaranteed fixed price contracts or nonguaranteed. In the former case, the funeral director guarantees to the purchaser that the price of the funeral to be provided in the future will not exceed the amount of funds paid on the contract plus any accruals thereon. If the contract is not guaranteed, the funeral director is only agreeing that amounts paid on the contract, plus accruals, will be applied toward the price of the future funeral. In the event that the price of the future funeral exceeds the amounts set aside to pay for it, the purchaser or the decedent's estate will have to make up the balance.

Another variable found in preneed contracts is the issue of revocability. Preneed contracts which are revocable may be terminated by the purchaser at any time prior to the death of the beneficiary with the purchaser receiving a refund of all or some part of the funds paid on the contract, plus all or some of the accruals thereon. The amount that is returned is often determined by state law. If the contract is irrevocable, the purchaser may not cancel it.

Although preneed contracts have existed for many years, it is only in the past twenty-five years that their use has been widespread. With many funeral directors now actively promoting preneed arrangements and with the emergence of national marketing programs sponsored by large insurance companies, funeral home chains and state funeral trade associations, the trend toward preneed has been explosive. It has been estimated that by the year 2000 funeral directors will be writing two million preneed contracts per year. Obviously, if this projection holds up, the number of preneed contracts written on an annual basis will soon surpass at-need contracts.

10.2 State Trust Laws

With the emergence of preneed funeral contracts, state legislatures became concerned with the opportunity for fraud that was inherent with these arrangements. Noting that the contractual obligations of the funeral director were often not performed for up to twenty years after they received payment, the legislatures enacted various provisions to ensure that sellers of preneed funeral contracts would have sufficient funds in the future to fulfill their contractual obligations. Typically, these laws require the seller of preneed funeral contracts to place all or some part of the preneed funds in a trust. When the contract beneficiary died and the funeral services were provided, the preneed funds could be withdrawn and paid to the funeral director.

Preneed trust laws and/or regulations have now been enacted in 47 states. Although the trend is toward requiring an amount less than 100% of the preneed funds and interest thereon to be trusted, approximately one-half of states still require that all preneed funds and the interest earned thereon must remain in trust until the death occurs. The laws also usually require the funds to be deposited in insured banks or savings and loan accounts. Some states permit funeral directors to commingle the preneed accounts into one master account so that greater returns can be realized.

Approximately half of the states require sellers of preneed funeral contracts to have licenses. In a handful of states only funeral directors may sell preneed. Therefore, in most states the market is open to third party sellers, especially cemeteries who seek to sell caskets and vaults to consumers on a preneed basis. These sellers often use aggressive marketing programs such as direct mail, telesales and door-to-door solicitation to promote their preneed contract sales.

Because trusting laws, especially 100% trusting laws, deprive preneed sellers of available income, these laws have been attacked by third party sellers as unconstitutional deprivations of property and the right to contract. In addition, some state laws which limit or restrict door-to-door and other means of direct solicitation have been challenged as unconstitutional infringements on free speech.

For the most part, the courts have upheld the validity of state preneed laws as legitimate exercises of police power. For example, in *Memorial Gardens Assoc., Inc. v. Smith*, 16 Ill.2d 116, 156 N.E.2d 587 (1959), third party sellers challenged the 95% trusting requirements of the Illinois preneed statute. Noting that the average time lapse of 29 years between payment and performance invited fraud, the court upheld the law as a reasonable regulation enacted in the public interest. The same result was reached in *Messerli v. Monarch Memorial Gardens*, 397 P.2d 34 (Idaho 1964), where the court upheld a 100% trusting requirement. The decision found that the Idaho preneed law was not unconstitutional even if it did deprive legitimate businesses of operating funds since it was a reasonable measure taken pursuant to the state's power to prevent fraud and deceit.

With regard to First Amendment claims, a federal district court has upheld a West Virginia preneed law against claims that it violated the right of free speech. The law in question banned uninvited door-to-door and telephone solicitation of preneed funeral contracts. The court, noting past incidences of fraud and undue influence by third party sellers, held that the state had a significant governmental interest in protecting the public from improper solicitation practices. Since the ban only restricted the time, place and manner of speech and not the content of speech, and since the preneed sellers had ample alternative means of solicitation (direct mail, mass advertisement), the court found that the solicitation restrictions were rationally related to a legitimate state purpose. *National Funeral Services, Inc. v. Rockefeller*, (1986, U.S. District Court of Southern District of West Va., unreported).

10.3 Preneed Funding By Insurance

Burial insurance policies have been in existence for many years. This form of insurance, which was especially popular in the South, is payable in services or merchandise or as a credit toward services or merchandise. The insurance as usually in the form of a contract in which the purchaser is to be provided a funeral and the proceeds cannot be used otherwise.

Funeral insurance, on the other hand, is life insurance which is used to fund a separate preneed contract. It is typically a life insurance policy with the funeral home being designated as the beneficiary or the assignee of the policy. The growth of funeral insurance as a funding mechanism for preneed contracts has increased dramatically in recent times as large life insurance companies have established national preneed programs.

Preneed funding through insurance rather than trusting does offer two distinct advantages. Most preneed insurance products offer some type of face amount escalator which increases the insurance payoff to meet inflation. Unlike preneed trusts where interest or income earned by the trust is taxable, the accrual in the face amount of the insurance policy is tax free. Not only does this result in tax savings, but it also relieves funeral directors and trustees of administrative costs.

The second primary advantage in funding through insurance is the receipt by the funeral director of upfront income to cover the cost of his preneed marketing program. Since in most cases the funeral director serves as the insurance agent, he is usually able to obtain a commission upon the execution of the policy. Unlike those situations where a funeral director has to trust 100% of the funds until a future date, this feature of insurance preneed funding provides the funeral director with immediate compensation to help him meet the cost of operating a preneed marketing program.

In every state, life insurance must only be sold through a licensed life insurance agent. In most states a funeral director may obtain such a license. However, a few states prohibit a funeral director from becoming a licensed insurance agent. Other states restrict the dollar amount of policies funeral directors may sell or provide that they may only sell policies where the proceeds are intended to be assigned as payment for preneed goods and services.

10.4   Taxation of Preneed Income

As stated earlier, accruals on preneed insurance policies are not taxed. However, interest or income paid on preneed trust funds deposited in banks or elsewhere is subject to federal income tax. Prior to 1987 there was a great uncertainty regarding who paid this tax: the funeral director, the purchaser of the preneed contract or the trustee of the preneed contract.

In late 1987, the Internal Revenue Service issued Revenue Ruling 87-127 to clarify the tax status of preneed trusts. The Ruling is controlling on all preneed contracts entered into after January 29, 1988. If the preneed contract was executed prior to that date, the taxpayer, whether the funeral director, preneed purchaser or trustee, may continue to use the same tax treatment that those trusts used in the past.

Although Revenue Ruling 87-127 has not been interpreted by the courts or the IRS, it is apparent that in almost all cases the purchaser of the contract will be responsible for the payment of tax on interest or income earned by the trust funds. The trustee, whether it is the bank holding the funds or the funeral director, will have to report to the purchaser the amount of income earned each year by the trust. That income must then be reported on the purchaser's annual tax returns.

When the funeral services are performed and the funeral director receives the preneed funds in payment, these funds and all accruals thereon represent ordinary income to the funeral director. Likewise, if a funeral director is permitted by law to retain part of the preneed funeral payments or interest thereon prior to performing the service, these receipts of principal and interest will also be reported as ordinary income.

10.5   Medicaid/SSI

In determining eligibility for Medicaid assistance from the state or Supplemental Security Income ("SSI") from the Social Security Administration, the government examines the resources and income of applicants. If those resources and income are below certain levels, the applicant is eligible for assistance. When determining the value of the applicant's resources, the Medicaid or SSI caseworker will exclude or not count certain assets. Preneed funeral funds may be viewed as one of the excludable assets if the preneed contract is properly constructed.

a. Irrevocable Preneed Funeral Contracts.

Under current law, all funds placed in a preneed trust by a funeral director to fund an irrevocable preneed contract which are specifically identified to cover future burial expenses are excluded from an applicant's resources. In most states, there is no dollar limitation on this exclusion. Therefore, SSI and Medicare applicants who are purchasing preneed funerals should be encouraged to enter into irrevocable preneed contracts so that the funds paid for the preneed arrangements will be excluded from their countable resources.

b. Burial Space Exclusion.

When a revocable preneed contract is used, it still is possible to exclude all or part of the preneed funds from being counted as a resource. Current law provides a burial space exclusion that excludes the value of gravesites, crypts, mausoleums, urns, vaults, caskets or other repositories which are customarily and traditionally used for the remains of deceased persons from an applicant's resources. This exclusion applies in both revocable and irrevocable situations and it has no dollar limitation.

In order for the burial space exclusion to apply, the applicant must own the gravesite, casket, vault, etc. It is not, however, necessary that the applicant have physical possession of the burial space items. It is sufficient if the preneed contract shows the applicant's ownership of the burial space items. The contract should state that the applicant has purchased the particular burial space item and it should list the price of each such item. It is not necessary that the item be in existence at the time of the purchase as long as the purchase itself is evident from the contract.

c. Burial Funds Exclusion.

In addition to the burial space exclusion, there is a burial fund exclusion which can exclude up to $1,500 that is designated to pay for funeral expenses. Funds set aside for burial include revocable burial contracts, burial trusts and separately identifiable assets which are clearly designated to cover expenses connected with the individual's burial, cremation or other funeral arrangements. This burial fund exclusion can be used to cover the cost of funeral services such as embalming, professional service fees, hearse costs, cremation fees, etc. which are not covered by the burial space exclusion.

If a revocable preneed contract is used, and the applicant wishes to exclude all of the preneed funds as a resource, it is necessary that the value of those items not covered by the unlimited burial space exclusion be no more than the $1,500 exclusion available under the burial fund exclusion. To the extent that these items exceed the $1,500 limitation, the excess will be counted as a resource of the applicant for Medicaid/SSI eligibility purposes.

10.6 FTC Door-to-Door Regulation

If a preneed sale takes place outside of the funeral establishment, it is very possible that the preneed sales activity is subject to the Federal Trade Commission's Cooling-Off Regulation for Door-to-Door Sales. This regulation mandates that all door-to-door sellers must notify their customers that they have the right to cancel the door-to-door transaction at any time prior to midnight of the third business day after the date of the transaction.

This regulation has a broad application because of the rather expansive definitions given the terms "door-to-door sales" and "consumer goods and services." A door-to-door sale is defined as a sale of consumer goods or services exceeding $25.00 in which the seller personally solicits the sale and the sale is made at a place other than the seller's place of business. This term applies regardless of whether the seller initiated the solicitation or whether he responded to the invitation of the buyer.

"Consumer goods and services" are any goods or services purchased, leased or rented primarily for personal, family or household purposes. According to the Federal Trade Commission, funeral transactions are included in this definition. Given these broad definitions, it is clear that preneed funeral sellers who conduct business away from their established place of business would be subject to the regulation.

There is one exception under the regulation which may exempt certain preneed funeral transactions from the regulation. The exemption applies if the door-to-door sales are made pursuant to prior negotiations which took place when the consumer visited a retail business establishment where the goods and services are offered for sale. For example, if a consumer visited the funeral establishment to make the initial contact and later the preneed arrangements were made at the consumer's home, the FTC's Door-to-Door Regulation would not apply. It should be noted that this exemption is only available if the initial negotiations are made pursuant to an in-person visit to the funeral establishment; a phone call is not sufficient.

If the regulation does apply to the preneed funeral transaction, the funeral director will be committing an unfair or deceptive act or practice if he does any of the following:

(a) Fails to provide the consumer with a copy of the contract, or if a contract does not exist, a receipt which is dated, contains the seller's name and address, and the following disclosure in 10 point bold-faced type:

"You, the Buyer, may cancel this transaction at any time prior to midnight of the third business day after the date of this transaction. See the attached notice of cancellation form for an explanation of this right."

On the contract, the above disclosure must be in close proximity to the signature line for the buyer. If a receipt is given, the disclosure must appear on the front of the receipt.

(b) Fails to furnish the consumer a fully completed copy of the Notice of Cancellation which must be attached to the contract or receipt and must be in 10 point bold-faced print. The seller must also retain a completed copy for himself. The Notice of Cancellation must be in the following form:

NOTICE OF CANCELLATION

(Date)_____

YOU MAY CANCEL THIS TRANSACTION WITHOUT ANY PENALTY OR OBLIGATION, WITHIN THREE BUSINESS DAYS FROM THE ABOVE DATE. IF YOU CANCEL, ANY PROPERTY TRADED IN, ANY PAYMENTS MADE BY YOU UNDER THE CONTRACT OR SALE, AND ANY NEGOTIABLE INSTRUMENT EXECUTED BY YOU WILL BE RETURNED WITHIN TEN BUSINESS DAYS FOLLOWING RECEIPT BY THE SELLER OF YOUR CANCELLATION NOTICE, AND ANY SECURITY INTEREST ARISING OUT OF THE TRANSACTION WILL BE CANCELLED. IF YOU CANCEL, YOU MUST MAKE AVAILABLE TO THE SELLER AT YOUR RESIDENCE, IN SUBSTANTIALLY AS GOOD CONDITION AS WHEN RECEIVED, ANY GOODS DELIVERED TO YOU UNDER THIS CONTRACT OR THE SALE; OR YOU MAY IF YOU WISH, COMPLY WITH THE INSTRUCTIONS OF THE SELLER REGARDING THE RETURN SHIPMENT OF THE GOODS AT THE SELLER'S EXPENSE AND RISK. IF YOU DO MAKE THE GOODS AVAILABLE TO THE SELLER AND THE SELLER DOES NOT PICK THEM UP WITHIN TWENTY DAYS OF THE DATE OF YOUR NOTICE OF CANCELLATION, YOU MAY RETAIN OR DISPOSE OF THE GOODS WITHOUT ANY FURTHER OBLIGATION. IF YOU FAIL TO MAKE THE GOODS AVAILABLE TO THE SELLER, OR IF YOU AGREE TO RETURN THE GOODS TO THE SELLER AND FAIL TO DO SO, THEN YOU REMAIN LIABLE FOR PERFORMANCE OF ALL OBLIGATIONS UNDER THE CONTRACT. TO CANCEL THIS TRANSACTION, MAIL OR DELIVER A SIGNED AND DATED

**COPY OF THIS CANCELLATION NOTICE OR ANY OTHER WRITTEN NO-
TICE OR SEND A TELEGRAM TO [name of seller] AT [address of seller's
place of business] NO LATER THAN MIDNIGHT OF _____
_____[date].**

I HEREBY CANCEL THIS TRANSACTION.

(Date)_____   _____

(Buyer's Signature)

    (c) Includes in any door-to-door contract or receipt a confession of judg-
ment or a waiver of the consumer's right of cancellation.

    (d) Fails to orally inform the consumer about his right of cancellation or
misrepresent that right in any way.

    (e) Fails or refuses to honor a valid notice of cancellation. If a valid
cancellation is received, all payments must be returned and all negotiable
instruments signed by the buyer must be cancelled within ten business days
after the notice of cancellation.

    (f) Transfers, sells or assigns a negotiable instrument signed by the
buyer to any third party within five business days of the transaction.

    (g) Fails, within ten days of cancellation, to notify the buyer whether
the seller intends to repossess any shipped goods.

Chapter Eleven

WAGE AND HOUR LAWS

11.1 Overview

The Fair Labor Standards Act ("FLSA") (29 USC §201 et seq.) covers three areas of employment law that are important to funeral service: minimum wage, overtime compensation, and equal pay.

11.2 Enforcement

The FLSA is administered and enforced by the Wage and Hour Division of the Department of Labor. The Wage and Hour Division's enforcement responsibilities are carried out by compliance officers stationed across the United States. These enforcement officers have the authority to conduct investigations and to gather data on wages, hours and other employment practices in order to determine compliance with the FLSA. Where violations are found, they may recommend changes in employment practices to bring an employer into compliance. Investigations may occur as a result of routine audits or on the basis of an employee complaint.

Willful violations of the Act may result in criminal prosecution by the Division. In addition to criminal actions, the Wage and Hour Division, as well as individual claimants, can institute a civil action in federal or state court for unpaid minimum wages or overtime pay. Funeral directors should be aware that it is a violation of the FLSA to terminate or in any way retaliate against an employee for filing a complaint or participating in an investigation of the Wage and Hour Division.

With regard to civil actions, a court may award unpaid wages and overtime pay for a backpay period of up to two years from the date the complaint is filed. In the case of a willful violation, the backpay period can extend to three years. A willful violation occurs when the employer willingly violates the Act or is in reckless disregard of it. In addition to backpay, the court can award private litigants their attorney fees. Finally, the court can award an additional amount as liquidated damages which is equal to the backpay amount. In other words, the court can double the backpay award.

11.3 Coverage under the FLSA

a. Employers.

Not all employers are covered by the Act. Since 1989, an enterprise is covered only if its gross annual sales exceed $362,000. For a funeral home,

71

all proceeds from cash advances are included as part of gross receipts. Therefore, even funeral homes doing as few as 70 services per year may be covered by the FLSA.

In addition, if gross annual sales exceed $500,000, the enterprise is covered by the FLSA and also must comply with the post-1990 minimum wage scale of $4.35 per hour. For those enterprises with gross annual sales between $362,000 and $500,000, they need only pay the pre-1990 minimum wage scale of $3.35 per hour.

b. Employees.

Full-time employees are generally protected by the overtime and minimum wage requirements of the FLSA unless they qualify under the so-called "white collar" exemptions. The four white collar exemptions are as follows:

(1) **Executive Employee**. In order to fall under the executive employee exemption, an employee's primary duty must consist of the management of the enterprise in which he is employed or of a customarily recognized department or subdivision of that enterprise. The employee must customarily and regularly direct the work of two or more other employees in the enterprise. Examples of executive employees in the funeral profession may include the general manager of the funeral home or a branch manager.

(2) **Administrators**. An employee can fall under the administrator exemption if his primary duty requires the exercise of discretion and independent judgment, and consists of the performance of office or non-manual work directly related to management policies or general business operations.

Generally, secretaries and clerical workers rarely fall under this exemption. Typically, an office manager or a personnel director would qualify for this exemption. The key determinant is whether the administrator has a wide degree of discretion in the performance of his job.

(3) **Professionals**. The standards for determining if an individual falls under the classification of a professional are as follows:

- The employee's primary duties consist of the performance of learned, artistic or educational matters;

- The employee's work requires the consistent exercise of discretion and judgment; or

- The employee's work is predominantly intellectual and varied in character and his output cannot be standardized in relationship to time.

Although a funeral director must undergo substantial specialized education and training, the Department of Labor has determined that funeral director employees cannot be classified as "professionals".

(4) **Commissioned Outside Salesmen**. An employee who customarily and regularly works away from the employer's place of business while making sales and obtaining orders for which consideration is paid on a commission basis is regarded as a commissioned salesman and is not subject to the minimum or overtime wage benefits of the FLSA.

It is apparent that most employees of funeral homes, with the exception of executives and high level administrators, will not qualify for the white collar exemptions. Therefore, most of the employees should be regarded as subject to minimum wage and overtime protection.

11.4 Independent Contractors

Many funeral homes utilize individuals to perform specialized services on an irregular basis. For example, the home may use pallbearers, trade embalmers, bookkeepers, and limousine drivers. An issue which often arises is whether these individuals are employees or independent contractors.

Generally, the Wage and Hour Division will consider such individuals to be employees in circumstances where the funeral home dictates the specific details of the individual's job performance. On the other hand, if the factual circumstances indicate that the person rendering services is an independent businessman performing those services without direct and close supervision of the funeral home, an independent contractor status can be supported.

In this regard, the Wage and Hour Division will look at the following four factors:

(1) Is the individual free to perform the services on the employer's premises or elsewhere?

(2) Is the individual in business and performing the same services for other companies?

(3) Is the individual free to set his or her own hours of work? and

(4) Does the individual provide his own equipment or tools?

In determining independent contractor status, all of the factors above are examined and balanced. Applying these factors to scenarios which may occur in a funeral home setting, it is safe to say that an independent hairdresser would probably qualify as an independent contractor. A pallbearer, on the other hand, would probably be regarded as a part-time employee. The determination of a trade embalmer would be a close question that would turn on the particular facts. Obviously, if the funeral home transports the body to the embalmer's place of business, there is an independent contractor relationship. However, if the embalmer is using the funeral home facilities and equipment, and he has no such equipment available, he may be regarded as an employee.

11.5 Recordkeeping

With regard to employees that are subject to minimum wage and overtime requirements, the following records must be maintained:

(1) Personal information such as name, address, and social security number.

(2) Hours and day when the workweek begins.

(3) The total hours worked each day and each workweek.

(4) The total daily and weekly straight time earnings.

(5) The regular hourly rate for any workweek when overtime is worked.

(6) The total overtime pay for each workweek.

(7) Any deductions from or additions to wages.

(8) The total wages paid each pay period.

(9) The date of payment and the pay period covered.

Records should be maintained for a three year period except for payroll records which are required to be retained for six years in compliance with the requirements of the Internal Revenue Code. The records do not have to be maintained in any particular form and it is not necessary to have a time clock.

11.6 Minimum Wage

Since 1991, the minimum wage has been $4.35 per hour. Funeral directors should be aware that in a few states the minimum wage standards may even be more strict than the Federal standards. When both State and Federal laws apply, the law setting the higher standard must be observed.

There are provisions under the FLSA that allows an employer to pay apprentices and disabled individuals a wage scale that is lower than minimum wage. However, in order to qualify for this special wage scale, an employer must apply and receive certification from the Wage and Hour Division.

11.7 Overtime Pay.

a. General Requirements

Regarding the overtime provisions of the FLSA, all full-time employees that are not covered by a white collar exemptions must be paid at not less than 1-1/2 times their regular rate of pay for all hours worked over 40 hours in a workweek. The FLSA does not require an employee to be paid every week. The employer may make wage and salary payments at other regular intervals such as every two weeks, every half month, or every month.

What the FLSA does require is that the minimum wage and any overtime pay required must be computed on a basis of hours worked each workweek standing alone. An employer cannot average the hours of work over two or more weeks. For example, an employer cannot decline to pay overtime to an employee who worked 50 hours for the first week of the pay period, but only 30 hours during the second week.

How is a workweek computed? A workweek is a regular recurring period of 168 hours in the form of 7 consecutive 24 periods. It need not be the same as the calendar week. It can start on any day at any hour. Once established, however, it cannot be changed unless the change is intended to be permanent.

In determining an employee's regular rate of pay, the following issues may arise:

(1) **Meals and Lodging**. When meals and lodging are customarily provided for the benefit of the employee, the reasonable cost or fair market value of the benefits are considered wages. However, if the facilities furnished by the employer are primarily for the employer's benefit instead of the worker's, their costs may not be considered as wages. The costs of furnishing sleeping quarters to employees who have no other home may generally be regarded as wages under the FLSA.

(2) **Bonuses**. Production bonuses, attendance bonuses and commissions are included in wages. Gifts and discretionary bonuses are generally not included as wages.

(3) **Expenses**. Reimbursement for expenses incurred for the employer's benefit are not included in wages.

(4) **Profit Sharing**. Profit sharing, welfare and thrift plan payments are not part of wages.

(5) **Vacation Pay**. Vacation, holiday and sick pay are not included as wages. Also, premiums paid for holiday, Saturday and Sunday work which is over the time and one-half pay scale is also not included in wages.

b. *Salaried Employees.*

Although an employee may be hired as a salaried worker, he is regarded for wage and hour purposes as an hourly employee unless he is covered by one of the white collar exemptions. For example, if a funeral home hires an employee for $20,000 per year, for wage and hour purposes he is being paid $400 per week or $10.00 per hour. For any workweek where he works in excess of 40 hours, he must be compensated time and one-half, or $15, for each hour over 40 hours.

    c. Variable Workweek Agreement.

    One alternative to the regular overtime requirements is the Variable Workweek Agreement. This is also known as a Fluctuating Workweek Agreement. The primary advantage to the Variable Workweek Agreement is that it permits an employer to pay half time for overtime rather than time and a half.

    A Variable Workweek Agreement must be in writing and signed by the employee. It must also guarantee the employee a base weekly salary regardless of the number of hours he works. For example, if the employee has a $400 guaranteed weekly salary, he must be paid $400 a week regardless of whether he works less than 40 hours.

    If an employee under a Variable Workweek Agreement works in excess of 40 hours, he is entitled to one half of his regular hourly rate as overtime compensation. The difficulty in administering a Variable Workweek Agreements is determining the employee's regular hourly rate. The regular hourly rate will fluctuate depending upon the number of hours that the employee works. To determine an employee's hourly rate, one must divide his guaranteed salary by the number of hours he worked during the particular work week.

    For example, if an employee is guaranteed $400 a week and he works 50 hours in particular work week, his hourly rate for that workweek is $8.00. As compensation for that workweek, he would receive his $400 guaranteed salary. In addition, he would receive one half of his regular hourly rate for that week as overtime compensation. In this case, the overtime compensation would be $4 per hour or $40 for the total of 10 hours overtime compensation. Thus, his gross pay for the week would $440.

    Variable Workweek Agreements are not without risk. Some regional offices of the Wage and Hour Division will challenge the agreements, especially if the employee's work hours do not vary from week to week. Other regional offices readily allow the Workweek Agreements as long as they are in writing and agreed to by the employee. Funeral homes may wish to check with the regional office in their area before proceeding with Variable Workweek Agreements.

11.8 Equal Pay Act

Under the Equal Pay Act, employers may not discriminate on the basis of sex by paying employees of one sex at rates lower than they pay employees of the opposite sex in the same establishment, for doing equal work on jobs requiring substantially equal skill, effort and responsibility, and which are performed under similar working conditions. The Equal Pay Act covers executive, administrative and professional employees who, as detailed above, are exempt from the minimum wage and overtime coverage of the FLSA.

The Equal Pay Act permits unequal pay if it can be shown that the wage differential is based on a seniority system, a merit system or on any other factor other than sex. Employers should know that violations of the Act are subject to backpay claims in the same manner as minimum wage and overtime pay violations of the FLSA.

11.9 Particular Wage and Hour Issues for Funeral Homes

a. Caretaker.

Oftentimes, a funeral home will have a widow or other elderly caretaker who lives at the funeral home. The caretaker may perform very light duties or no duties at all. His primary purpose is to provide security for the funeral home and perhaps to answer the phones during off-hours.

The problem presented by the caretaker is whether the caretaker is an hourly employee that must be compensated for each hour he is at the funeral home. The Department of Labor has attempted to address issues such as this one with the following regulation:

> "An employee who resides on his employer's premises on a permanent basis for an extended period of time is not considered as working all the time he is on the premises. Ordinarily, he may engage in normal private pursuits and thus have enough time for eating, sleeping and entertaining and other periods of complete freedom from all duties when he may leave the premises for the purposes of his own. It is of course difficult to determine the exact hours worked under these circumstances and any reasonable agreement of the parties which takes into consideration all of the pertinent facts will be accepted."

As the above regulation shows, an individual is not deemed to be working simply because he is on the premises. Presumably, the elderly caretaker would only be working during the time that he was performing light duties or answering the telephone for the funeral home. Technically, the caretaker should thus be paid at least the minimum wage for the time he responds to telephone calls and performs light duties. However, funeral homes may offset those wages in exchange for the free lodging which is provided the caretaker.

To protect the funeral home, it is recommended that the caretaker of the funeral home enter into a simple agreement by which the caretaker agrees to answer the phone and perform other specified light duties in exchange for free lodging. An alternative to this would be to pay the caretaker minimum wage for his actual working time.

b. On Call Employees.

Funeral homes often require their employees to be on call so that they may respond to death calls. An issue which often arises is whether the on call employee must be compensated for the time he is on call but away from the funeral home premises.

Generally, employees who are required to be on call will not be considered to be working if the arrangement with the employer is considered to be one in which the employee is "waiting to be engaged." On the other hand, the employee will be considered to be working for the entire period if it is determined that he is "engaged to wait."

The determination of whether an employee is "waiting to be engaged" or "engaged to wait" turns on the freedom of the employee to engage in personal activities. To the extent that the arrangement substantially restricts any movement by the employee, there is an issue as to whether or not he is working during the waiting period.

If, for example, an employee was required to man the telephone at the funeral home and could not leave the funeral home premises, he would be regarded as being "engaged to wait." If, however, the telephone could be put on call forwarding to his home and he could engage in personal pursuits, although he still had to remain at home, the issue is a much closer question.

The best solution to the on-call issue is to provide beepers to on-call employees so that their freedom of movement is not restricted. If that is not possible, funeral directors should at least have call forwarding so that employees can be at home doing personal activities. Assuming they are not on-call an inordinate amount of time, and agree that this on-call status constitutes waiting to be engaged, the funeral home may be able to withstand any subsequent challenges by the Wage and Hour Division.

Chapter Twelve

FEDERAL EMPLOYMENT LAW

12.1 Introduction

In addition to the Wage and Hour laws, two other federal statutes place substantial regulatory responsibilities on the funeral director in his role as employer. Correspondingly, these statutes provide significant protections to funeral directors and others who are funeral home employees or applicants for employment. Therefore, whether the funeral director is in the role of employer or employee, these statutes can have a direct impact on his or her employment relationship.

12.2 Americans with Disabilities Act

a. Overview.

In Chapter Nine there was an examination of how the Americans with Disabilities Act ("ADA") requires funeral homes as public accommodations to make their facilities accessible to disabled members of the public. The ADA also impacts funeral homes as employers by imposing detailed regulations on the treatment of employees and applicants for employment who have disabilities.

b. Coverage of ADA.

Funeral homes that employ 15 or more employees fall under the coverage of the employment-related provisions of the ADA. Funeral homes with less than 15 employees are exempt from the ADA's employment-related provisions.

With funeral homes often employing part-time and casual labor, how does a funeral home determine the number of employees it has? Generally, if a funeral home employs 15 or more employees for each working day in each of 20 or more calendar weeks in the current or the preceding calendar year, it will be covered by the employment provisions of the ADA. Therefore, funeral directors may have to make a detailed examination of past employment records to determine if they are covered by this section of the ADA. In making the determination, it is necessary to include all employees, part-time and casual, in the calculation.

c. Purpose of the ADA.

Generally, the purpose of the employment provisions of the ADA is to prohibit employers from discriminating against disabled individuals in all

79

phases of the employment relationship — job application and testing procedures, hiring, advancement, discharge, compensation, and job training. This does not mean that an employee with a disability is to be given preference over one without disabilities. The ADA does not establish quotas or preferences. It merely prohibits the employer from considering the fact that an individual is disabled in making certain employment decisions.

In a nutshell, the ADA protects "qualified individuals with a disability." In order to be a qualified individual with a disability, the employee must be able to perform the "essential functions" of the job with or without "reasonable accommodations." Employers are required by the ADA to supply reasonable accommodations on the job to a disabled individual unless to do so would constitute an "undue hardship."

As evident from the above summary of the ADA's employment-related provisions, whether the ADA applies in many employment decisions will turn upon how subjective terms such as "disability", "essential functions", "reasonable accommodations", and "undue hardship" are defined. While the regulations issued by the Equal Employment Opportunity Commission ("EEOC") to interpret this part of the ADA give some guidance, in many situations the precise scope of these terms must be decided on a case-by-case basis.

d. Disability.

A "disability" is any physical or mental impairment that substantially limits one or more life activities, a record of having such an impairment, or being regarded as having such an impairment. Mental and physical impairments can include mental retardation; organic brain syndrome; emotional or mental illness; special learning disabilities; orthopaedic, visual, speech and hearing impairment; cerebral palsy; epilepsy; muscular dystrophy; multiple sclerosis; HIV infection; cancer; heart disease; diabetes; cosmetic disfigurement; anatomical loss; drug addiction; and alcoholism.

Although drug addiction and alcoholism are disabilities, individuals currently taking illegal drugs or alcohol are not protected by the ADA. Also, the definition of disability does not include homosexuality or bisexuality; transvestism, exhibitionism, gender identity disorders, or other sexual behavior disorders; compulsive gambling; kleptomania; or pyromania.

There are two steps involved in determining whether an individual is a "qualified individual with a disability." First, this determination concerns whether the individual has the prerequisites for the position to be filled, such as appropriate educational background, employment experience, skills, or licenses. The second determination to be made is whether or not the individual can perform the essential functions of the position with or without reasonable accommodations.

These two determinations must be made at the time the employer is making the employment decision. The employer cannot base his decision on speculation regarding the employee's future inability to perform the job, the risk the employee may become disabled in the future, or the potential increase in health insurance cost which may result from the employee's disability.

e. *Essential Functions.*

In order to determine if an individual can perform the essential functions of a job, it is imperative to first know what those functions are. Understandably, the EEOC did not attempt to define those functions for each of the hundreds of occupations that exist today. Rather, the EEOC has indicated that it will look in the first instance to the employer's judgment as to what functions of a particular job are essential. However, in order for the employer's list of essential functions to be considered as evidence, the list must be prepared in written form PRIOR to the advertising of the job opening or the interviewing of job applicants.

In drafting the list of the essential functions of a job, what factors should be considered by the employer? Generally, essential functions are job duties that are fundamental and not marginal. Factors to be considered are:

- The importance of the function to the overall job.

- Whether there are other employees who can perform the function in question.

- Whether the function is so highly specialized that the employee must perform it because of his particular expertise or ability.

- What is the relative amount of time that an employee holding the position would spend performing the particular function?

- What are the consequences of having other employees perform the function or of not having the function performed at all?

- Do current holders of the job perform the function and, if so, how much time do they spend performing that function?

In interviewing all job applicants, the employer would provide the applicant with the written list of the essential functions of the job and ask the applicant whether he or she can perform each of the essential functions with or without a reasonable accommodation. Generally, it is the responsibility of the job applicant or the disabled employee to inform the employer that an accommodation is needed. Once the employer has learned that an accommodation is needed, the employer and the employee/applicant should meet to determine: (1) what are the precise job-related limitations imposed by the applicant/employee's disability and how these limitations can be overcome; (2) what potential accommodations are available and what will be their effectiveness in enabling the individual to perform the essential functions of the job; and (3) what are the individual's accommodation preferences?

It is, of course, impossible to list all possible accommodations which could or may be made. However, examples of the types of accommodations which may have to be made include the following: installing ramps, modifying work areas and restrooms so they are accessible; job restructuring; modified work schedules; reassignment to vacant positions; permitting the use of accrued paid leave or providing additional unpaid leave for necessary treatment; providing reserved parking spaces; and acquiring or modifying equipment or devices such as page turners, lifting devices, telephone handset amplifiers, telecommunication devices for deaf persons, and raised or lowered furniture.

Employers should note that a reasonable accommodation need not be the best accommodation possible, but must sufficiently meet the job-related needs of the individual being accommodated. Furthermore, the employer is generally not required to provide a disabled employee with accommodations that are primarily for the personal benefit of the disabled individual such as one that assists the individual throughout his daily activities both on and off the job. For example, an employer is generally not required to provide a disabled employee with artificial limbs, wheelchairs or eyeglasses.

f. Undue Hardship.

The failure to provide reasonable accommodations may be justified where the employer can demonstrate that the accommodation would impose an undue hardship on the operation of its business. Of course, for an accommodation to constitute an undue hardship it must require more than a "de minimis" expense or inconvenience.

Whether a reasonable accommodation imposes an undue hardship on an employer must be determined on a case-by-case basis. Obviously, what is an undue hardship for a small employer may not be an undue hardship for a large scale employer. The following 11 factors are relevant in determining whether an undue hardship exists:

- The importance of the function to the overall job.

- The nature and cost of the accommodation required;

- The overall financial resources of the facility involved in the provision of the reasonable accommodation;
- The number of the persons employed at the facility;
- The effect of the reasonable accommodation on expenses and resources;
- The impact of the accommodation on the operation of the facility;
- The overall resources of the employer;
- The overall size of the employer's business with respect to the number of employees;
- The number, type and location of its facilities;
- The type of operation of the employer, including the composition, structure and function of its workforce;
- The geographic separateness of the facility; and
- The administrative or fiscal relationship of the facility to the employer.

The concept of undue hardship takes into account not only financial difficulties but any substantial or disruptive interference caused by the accommodation. For example, if an employee requested the employer to raise the thermostat as an accommodation, such an accommodation may create an undue hardship for other employees, patrons or customers. In such a case, the employer would be justified in refusing the accommodation.

12.3 Civil Rights Laws

a. Overview.

Title VII of the Civil Rights Act of 1964, 42 USC §2000 et seq. (as amended), prohibits discriminatory practices in employment based on race, color, religion, sex, or national origin. Title VII was amended in 1978 by the Pregnancy Discrimination Act which makes it unlawful for an employer to discriminate against a pregnant woman in employment decisions. Another important protection for employees was provided by the Age Discrimination in Employment Act ("ADEA") 29 USC §621 et seq. (as amended), which prohibits an employer from refusing to hire, discharging, denying employment, or making any employment decision on the basis of an individual's age. The ADEA provides protection only to those who are forty years or older.

b. Coverage of the Civil Rights Laws.

The Civil Rights Act, including the Pregnancy Discrimination Act, applies to all employers having 15 or more employees. The coverage of the

ADEA is restricted to employers with 20 or more employees. To determine whether part-time or casual labor should be counted, funeral homes should utilize the same test that applies under the employment related sections of the ADA. Therefore, if the funeral home employs 15 or more employees for each working day in each of 20 or more calendar weeks in the current or preceding calendar year, it will be covered by the Civil Rights Act. (The threshold for the ADEA is 20 employees).

Although funeral homes with less than 15 employees are exempt from the Civil Rights Act, it must be pointed out that 45 states have enacted laws which are similar or even go beyond the Civil Rights Act in protecting employees. And, as a general rule, most of these state laws cover all employers in the state. Therefore, although smaller funeral homes may be exempt from the Civil Rights Act, they are probably subject to similar restrictions under state law.

c. Scope of the Civil Rights Laws.

The trio of Civil Rights Laws generally prohibit an employer from basing employment-related decisions on race, color, religion, sex, national origin, pregnancy or age. Prior to 1991, if an employer could show that although an impermissible factor had entered into an employment decision, the same decision would have been made based on other permissible factors, then no violation of the Civil Rights Act occurred. However, with the amendment of the Civil Rights Act in 1991, if there is any showing that a discriminatory motive entered into the decision, a violation of the Civil Rights Act has taken place.

Because of the 1991 amendments to the law, it is vital for employers to institute safeguards against impermissible motives becoming part of employment-related decisions. This is especially true in hiring employees. It is critical that employers utilize employment applications that have been reviewed for any inquires into race, religion, age, national origin, sex, and disabilities. Equally important, the representative of the employer conducting the interview of applicants must be trained to avoid any discussions of these prohibited topics.

Decisions regarding promotions, compensation, benefits, discipline, and discharges must also be made without regard to any of the prohibited factors. Employers now routinely utilize employment manuals, periodic written employee evaluations, and detailed employment files to protect themselves against claims under these statutes. Generally, the wisest advice to employers is to thoroughly document all employment related decisions so that there is a written record of why and how the decision was made.

d. Enforcement.

Title VII of the Civil Rights Act is enforced by the Equal Employment Opportunity Commission ("EEOC"). The EEOC carries out its mission through a two-step process — mediation and enforcement.

Whenever an employee or a job applicant feels he was a victim of discrimination, he must first file a claim with the EEOC or similar state agency before proceeding to court. That charge must generally be filed within six months of the alleged discriminatory practice. The EEOC will alert the employer of the charge and begin a broad investigation. Generally, the investigator will interview the charging party and his witnesses. He will then interview the employer and any witnesses he may have. An investigation may include an on-site tour with an interview of other employees. Employers will also generally be requested to produce payroll records, timesheets, seniority lists, job descriptions, employee manuals and handbooks and personnel records.

Within 120 days after the charge is filed with the EEOC, the investigator will make a determination of "cause" or "no cause". If a no cause determination is made, the EEOC charge is dismissed. The complainant then receives a Right-to-Sue letter which allows him 90 days in which to file a private action in federal court.

If the EEOC finds that there is cause to believe a violation of Title VII has occurred, it will attempt to work out a settlement between the complainant and the employer. If this consultation process is not fruitful, the EEOC can file an action in federal district court or can issue a Right-to-Sue letter to the complainant so that he can sue in federal court.

Because of the EEOC's broad investigatory powers, it is important for funeral directors to maintain clean paper trails. The EEOC requires all employers to maintain for at least six months after any personnel action all records related to such action, such as employment application forms, hiring records, demotions, promotions, transfers, layoffs, and termination records, pay rates and training and apprentice selection records. It is generally recommended to employers that all such records be maintained for up to three years.

Chapter Thirteen

OCCUPATIONAL SAFETY AND HEALTH ACT

13.1 Overview

In 1970, Congress enacted the Occupational Safety and Health Act. That Act created the Occupational Safety and Health Administration ("OSHA") within the Department of Labor. OSHA has been charged with the responsibility to protect the nation's employees by implementing new safety and health programs, providing research into occupational safety, instituting a reporting and recordkeeping system to track job related injuries and illness, establish training programs, and develop and enforce mandatory job safety and health standards.

In general, OSHA extends to all employers in the 50 states, the District of Columbia and all other territories under federal government jurisdiction. Coverage is provided directly by federal OSHA or through an OSHA-approved state program. Approximately half of the states conduct OSHA-approved state programs.

Any person or business that is engaged in business and has employees is subject to OSHA. However, OSHA does not cover self-employed persons. Therefore, if a funeral home is a sole proprietorship with the owner serving as the only employee, the funeral home would not be subject to OSHA requirements.

13.2 Enforcement

To enforce its standards, OSHA is authorized under the Act to conduct workplace inspections. OSHA compliance officers will conduct the inspection. Typically, such inspections can be triggered by fatal accidents on the job site, employee complaints, or random inspections of any industry that OSHA is targeting. Following the inspection, the OSHA officer will conduct a closing conference with the employer to discuss all unsafe or unhealthful conditions observed on the inspection. At this time, all apparent violations for which a citation may be issued are discussed. The compliance officer will submit a report to the OSHA area director with a recommendation as to proposed penalties.

The area director may issue citations and propose penalties for those citations. When issued a citation or notice of a proposed penalty, an employer may request an informal meeting with the OSHA's area director to discuss the case. If the employer does not contest the citation, the employer must correct the cited hazard by the prescribed date.

13.3 Notice and Recordkeeping

All employers, including funeral homes, must display OSHA's job safety and health protection workplace poster 2203, or its state equivalent. The poster should be predominately displayed on the bulletin board utilized for employee notices.

As a service industry, funeral homes are exempt from OSHA's basic recordkeeping requirements. These recordkeeping requirements involve the maintenance of OSHA Form 200 which is a basic log and summary of occupational illnesses and injury. OSHA Form 101 is used to supply supplementary information regarding each injury and illness noted on the log. Unless a particular funeral home has been notified by the Bureau of Labor Statistics that it must maintain these records, funeral homes are exempt from these requirements. However, funeral homes in those states with state-approved OSHA plans may have to maintain these basic recordkeeping requirements. In addition, many funeral homes voluntarily maintain these forms.

In the event of an accident at the funeral home involving the death of an employee or the hospitalization of five or more employees, the employer must report the accident to the local or regional OSHA office within 48 hours of the accident. The report must explain the circumstances of the accident, the number of fatalities, if any, and the extent of any injuries.

13.4 General Requirements Standard

As employers, funeral homes are subject to the same general requirements that apply to all other employers subject to OSHA. These requirements are extremely detailed and complex. They regulate items such as the number and placement of fire extinguishers, the posting and lighting of exits, the installation, marking and grounding of electrical equipment and outlets, the width, depth, texture and angle of walking and working surfaces, guards and other protective devices required for the use of machinery and powered lift platforms, and numerous other labels, warnings and signs which must be posted throughout the working environment.

13.5 Specific OSHA Standards Applicable to Funeral Homes

In addition to the general requirements regulations which all employers must comply with, funeral directors are subject to three specific OSHA standards — the Formaldehyde Exposure Standard, the Hazard Communication Standard, and the Bloodborne Pathogen Standard. Each of these standards require affirmative steps and programs which the funeral home must undertake in order to maintain compliance. Although there is some overlap in the requirements of these standards, the funeral director must have a working knowledge of each standard in order to pass an OSHA inspection.

13.6 Formaldehyde Exposure Standard

a. Overview.

The Formaldehyde Exposure Standard took effect in 1988. The purpose of this standard is to establish permissible exposure levels for formaldehyde in the workplace. This purpose is accomplished by three basic exposure levels. The first level is the 8-hour Time Weighted Average ("TWA") of .75 parts per million ("ppm"). The second level is the 15-minute Short Term Exposure Level ("STEL") of 2 ppm. Finally, there is the Action Level. If the 8-hour TWA is .5 ppm, the employer has exceeded the Action Level and is required to take certain remedial steps.

Every funeral director with employees is required to conduct formaldehyde monitoring of the preparation room. The 8-hour TWA monitoring should be conducted during peak activities at the preparation room. Of course, the STEL monitoring is to be done during an embalming.

Funeral directors are required to notify employees in writing of the results of the monitoring within 15 days of receiving those results. Retesting should be done whenever changes are made in personnel, equipment or other areas that may cause levels of formaldehyde to increase. All monitoring results should be placed in permanent records.

b. On-going Compliance Responsibilities.

If the monitoring reports show that the STEL is below 2 ppm and the TWA is below the Action Level of .5 ppm, the funeral home is not required to take any remedial action. However, the funeral home still has to comply with seven on-going responsibilities under the Formaldehyde Exposure Standard. Those responsibilities are as follows:

(1) **Protective Equipment and Clothing**. Funeral homes must provide protective clothing and equipment to their employees to guard against skin absorption or physical contact with formaldehyde. The equipment must be provided at no cost to the employees. The employer must require that the clothing is worn by any employee that has a potential of coming in contact with formaldehyde.

Protective equipment includes rubber or disposable latex gloves, chemical resistant gowns, goggles, face shields, head and shoe covers, and chemical resistant aprons. Any clothing becoming contaminated must be cleaned or stored with adequate warning so that those who handle it know it is contaminated.

(2) **Hygiene Protection**. Funeral homes must provide change rooms for employees to change from work clothes to protective clothes. In addition, "quick drench" showers must be available in the prep room for any employees who become exposed to formaldehyde. Showers must be in the immediate vicinity of the work area and have the capability to drench the employee quickly and for a continual 15 to 20 minute period. There must also be eye wash facilities readily available. Eye wash squeeze bottles are not sufficient under the standard.

(3) **Housekeeping**. Funeral homes must institute a visual inspection system of the preparation room to detect any spills or leaks. Of course, all spills and leaks are to be promptly cleaned up by employees wearing protective gear. Formaldehyde waste should be disposed of in sealed containers with warning labels. A written record of inspections and repairs must be maintained.

(4) **Emergencies**. Funeral homes must institute procedures to follow in the event of an emergency due to formaldehyde exposure.

(5) **Hazard Communication**. Funeral homes must assemble Material Safety Data Sheets ("MSDS") on formaldehyde and provide these to the employees. The collection of MSDS is discussed further in Section 13.7.

(6) **Employee Training**. Employees must be trained on the proper use of protective clothing and gear, the cleaning-up of spills, the proper handling of formaldehyde, and emergency procedures.

(7) **Recordkeeping**. All applicable records, including the monitoring records, must be maintained for 30 years. Employees should certify that they have received training and a written report of the formaldahyde monitoring results.

c. Remedial Measures.

If the monitoring of the preparation room shows that the STEL level is below 2 ppm and the TWA level is below .75 ppm, but above the .5 ppm Action Level, the funeral home is required to take the following three remedial steps:

(1) **Formaldehyde Exposure Reduction**. The funeral home shall institute immediate steps to reduce formaldehyde exposure. This can be done by the adoption of safe working practices, the rearrangement of the room so that formaldehyde fumes flow away from the embalmer, and/or the installation of additional ventilation fans.

(2) **Periodic Monitoring**. The funeral home must repeat the formaldehyde monitoring at least every six months until the exposure level falls below the Action Level.

(3) **Medical Surveillance**. The funeral home must institute medical surveillance of employees who are exposed to formaldehyde. This requires a medical questionnaire to be answered by the employees under the supervision of a doctor. The questionnaire lists the employee's work history, information about smoking, medical problems, skin problems, etc. If the physician believes there may be an exposure problems based on the questionnaire, he or she is to give a medical exam to the employee. A copy of the physician's written medical opinion is to be provided to the employee and one copy is to be maintained in the employer's records for 30 years.

d. Additional Remedial Steps.

If the formaldehyde monitoring shows that the level exceeds the STEL of 2 ppm or the TWA of .75 ppm, the funeral home is required to institute three more additional remedial steps:

(1) **Written Plan**. The funeral home shall prepare a written plan for the immediate reduction of exposure levels.

(2) **Posting of Warnings**. The funeral home shall post warnings on the door of the preparation room alerting anyone who enters about the dangers of formaldehyde.

(3) **Respirators**. If the formaldehyde level cannot be reduced immediately, the funeral home shall provide respirators and institute a respirator program.

13.7 Hazard Communication Standard

The Hazard Communication Standard also took effect in 1988. It is basically a disclosure law so that employees are provided information regarding the hazardous materials with which they are working. There are four basic requirements to the Hazard Communication Standard. They are as follows:

(1) **Material Safety Data Sheets**. Funeral homes are required to obtain and maintain Material Safety Data Sheets ("MSDS") from all manufacturers of products used or stored at the funeral home that contain hazardous substances. A Material Safety Data Sheet contains a full disclosure of the product's hazards, precautions in handling the product, and proper steps to take in the event of an emergency.

The funeral home must obtain a Material Safety Data Sheet for each hazardous product. The data sheets are to be placed in a three ring binder which is identified as the "MSDS" binder. The sheets are to be arranged in alphabetical order by product name. An index of the products should be prepared and placed in the front of the binder. An MSDS binder should be placed in the preparation room in a designated area with a copy of the MSDS binder in the main office of the funeral home.

(2) **Container Labeling**. All containers of hazardous products must be labeled with the name of the product, appropriate hazard warnings, and the name and address of the manufacturer. Typically, most hazardous products are already labeled by the manufacturer to comply with these requirements.

If the funeral home were to transfer a product from the manufacturer's container into its own container, the funeral home must relabel the new container. The only exception to this requirement is when the product is placed in a container of 10 gallons or less and used immediately.

(3) **Employee Training**. The funeral home must develop a written hazard communication training and information program for its employees. The program shall be provided for all new employees and repeated whenever a new hazard is introduced into the work area. The program should include information on the labeling of containers containing hazardous substances, the data that is contained on a MSDS, the location of the MSDS binder, the safe handling of hazardous materials, the wearing of protective equipment and clothing, the proper clean-up of hazardous materials, the actions that are to be taken in the event of an emergency, the requirements of the Hazard Communication Standard, and the location and availability of the funeral home's written program for compliance with the Hazard Communication Standard. Employees who have undertaken the training should execute certifications indicating when the training was received.

(4) **Hazard Communication Program**. The funeral home must institute a written Hazard Communication Program which outlines how the funeral home intends to comply with the requirements of the Hazard Communication Standard. The program must be maintained and made available to all employees.

13.8   Bloodborne Pathogen Standard

In 1988, OSHA instituted an interim Bloodborne Pathogen Standard. That standard became final in 1993. The standard contains the following six compliance requirements:

(1) **Exposure Control Plan**. The funeral home must draft a written Exposure Control Plan which explains how the funeral home intends to institute safe work habits and housekeeping practices to minimize exposure to bloodborne pathogens. The plan must include a discussion of the job classifications in which employees have exposure to bloodborne pathogens, how the funeral home intends to implement precautions, training, recordkeeping and hepatitis B vaccine procedures, and the procedure for evaluating exposure incidents.

(2) **Hepatitis B Vaccination**. Funeral homes must make hepatitis B vaccine and vaccination series available to employees who have exposure to bloodborne pathogens. The vaccination must be made available at no cost to employees and at a reasonable time and place.

(3) **Protective Equipment and Clothing**. As with the other standards, the funeral home is required to maintain and supply protective clothing and equipment for employees that have occupational exposure.

(4) **Training Program**. Each employee with potential occupational exposure must complete a training program when initially hired and annually thereafter. Training sessions must be conducted by individuals with expertise in this area. The training shall include discussions of the Bloodborne Pathogen Standard, a general explanation of bloodborne pathogens and related diseases, the modes of transmission, the use and limitations of personal protective clothing and equipment, safe work practices, information concerning the hepatitis B immunization program and an explanation of signs and labels. All employees who undergo the training should certify when and under conditions they receive training.

(5) **Exposure Incidents**. In the event of an exposure to blood or other potentially infectious material, the employer must make available to the exposed employee post-exposure evaluation and follow up.

(6) **Recordkeeping**. Training records must be maintained for 5 years. Medical records for an employee must be maintained for 30 years after the employment relationship ends. Each employee should have a medical records file containing his or her name, social security number, hepatitis B vaccination, record of exposure incidents, and medical evaluations.

Chapter Fourteen

FTC FUNERAL RULE

14.1 Introduction

In 1984, the Federal Trade Commission ("FTC") put into effect the Funeral Industry Practices Trade Regulation Rule (16 C.F.R. Part 453). That regulation, which is commonly referred to as the Funeral Rule, was reviewed and revised in 1994.

The primary purposes of the Funeral Rule are threefold: (1) to give consumers the right to select those funeral goods and services which they wish to purchase; (2) to provide consumers access to detailed, itemized price information prior to purchase decisions; and (3) to prevent misrepresentations and other unfair and deceptive practices in the sale of funeral goods and services.

The Funeral Rule seeks to obtain its objectives by requiring funeral directors to distribute to consumers a series of price lists and documents at various stages of funeral arrangements. These lists must contain itemized prices of the various components of a funeral. Also included in the lists are mandatory printed disclosures informing consumers of the practical and legal necessity of certain funeral goods and services.

Any entity that offers to sell or that does sell funeral goods and funeral services is subject to the Funeral Rule. It is important to note that the Rule covers only those that sell both funeral goods and services. Therefore, if a cemetery sells only caskets and vaults, but does not offer funeral services (care of the body, direction of funeral ceremonies), it is not subject to the Rule.

14.2 General Price List

The cornerstone of the Funeral Rule is the General Price List ("GPL"). The GPL is given to the consumer prior to the purchase of the funeral and provides him with a detailed itemized listing of the goods and services offered by the funeral home.

a. Introductory Matters.

On the General Price List, the funeral home must place its name, address, telephone number, the words "General Price List" and the effective date of the General Price List.

95

b. Itemization of Sixteen Goods and Services.

To insure that consumers have the right to pick and choose those items which they wish to purchase, the Federal Trade Commission has selected sixteen various funeral goods and services that must be separately priced on the GPL. It is important to note that funeral homes are only required to list these goods and services if they offer them for sale. For example, if a funeral home elects not to offer direct cremation, it may be deleted from the General Price List.

Funeral homes will typically sell additional goods and services other than the sixteen which must be separately itemized. While funeral homes are not required to place other goods and services on the GPL, as a matter of proper business practice, it is recommended that all goods and services offered by the funeral home be listed on the GPL.

The following is a list of the sixteen goods and services that must be separately itemized on the GPL:

(1) **Basic Services of Funeral Director and Staff**. The basic service fee of the funeral director is the only fee on the General Price List that may be made non-declinable. In other words, the funeral home can require a consumer to pay this charge as a condition of obtaining a funeral. The basic service fee is to include those services that are furnished by a funeral director in arranging nearly any funeral, such as conducting the arrangement conference, planning the funeral, obtaining necessary permits, shelter of remains, and placement of obituary notices. This fee may also include any charges for the recovery of funeral home overhead such as utility expenses, secretarial and administrative costs, equipment and inventory expenses.

(2) **Embalming**. The second mandatory price listing on the GPL is the charge for embalming. In addition to the embalming charge, some funeral directors will list additional charges for embalming autopsy cases or tissue donations. This is permissible. (As indicated in Chapter Nine, there cannot be an additional charge for the embalming of contagious diseases cases.)

(3) **Other Preparation of the Body**. Under this category, the funeral home should list any other fees charged in preparing the body. Typical examples include dressing and casketing, hair styling, washing or disinfecting unembalmed remains, and refrigeration charges.

(4) **Services and Facilities for Viewing**. In charging for a visitation, the funeral home should list a fee that covers the services of the funeral director and staff during the visitation as well as the use of facilities. Under this category, funeral homes may have a series of visitation charges. For example, some firms charge according to the length of the visitation (half day, one day, two day) or whether the visitation is pubic or private.

96

(5) **Services and Facilities for Funeral Ceremony.** As with visitation, the funeral home should list the price of the funeral ceremony. Some funeral homes will list several charges under this category depending upon whether the funeral is conducted at the funeral home or at another location such as a church.

(6) **Services and Facilities for Memorial Service**. A memorial service is a ceremony without the body present. If offered by a funeral home, the funeral home is required to list the price of the service on the General Price List.

(7) **Service and Equipment for Graveside Service**. A graveside funeral service is a ceremony at the graveside when no other funeral ceremony is conducted by the funeral home. This should be distinguished from a committal service which may be included as part of the funeral ceremony. In quoting the price of the graveside funeral service, the charge should include all services and equipment the funeral home will utilize in performing the service.

(8) **Transfer of Remains to Funeral Home**. This charge may be a flat, hourly, or a mileage charge. Many funeral directors impose a flat fee within a certain radius and an excess mileage charge outside of the radius. All charges related to this service, whether it is the use of the hearse or the staff time involved in performing the transfer, must be included in this one charge.

(9) **Hearse**. Fees for the use of the hearse must be separately itemized. At the option of the funeral home, this charge may be a flat fee, a mileage fee, or an hourly fee.

(10) **Limousine**. As with the hearse, the limousine charge may be a flat, hourly or mileage fee.

(11) **Casket Price Range**. If a funeral home has a separate Casket Price List from its General Price List, it must provide a casket price range of its highest and lowest price casket offerings on the GPL.

(12) **Outer Burial Container Price Range**. As with caskets, if the funeral home maintains a separate Outer Burial Container Price List from its GPL, it must include on the GPL the price range of its highest and lowest price outer burial containers. If the funeral home chooses not to have separate price lists for caskets and outer burial containers, it should list all casket and vault offerings on the General Price List.

(13) **Forwarding of Remains**. The forwarding of remains is one of the four dispositions/funeral services (together with receiving remains, direct cremation and immediate burial) that the Funeral Rule requires funeral homes to present as a package to consumers. In other words, one price should be

presented under this listing which will inform the consumer of the total price of forwarding remains. For this reason, a funeral home is required to group all charges relating to this service (service fee, transportation, embalming) into one charge.

(14) **Receiving Remains**. As with forwarding remains, this package offering must present one price to the consumer that covers all components of the receiving of remains from another funeral home.

(15) **Direct Cremation**. A direct cremation is a disposition of human remains by cremation without formal viewing, visitation or any other ceremony with the body present. If a funeral home offers direct cremation, it is obligated to list it as a package on the GPL. In addition, the funeral home is required to offer several package offerings under direct cremation. For example, the funeral home must quote the price of a direct cremation if the consumer elects to utilize his own container and the price of a direct cremation if the consumer purchases a container from the funeral home. If a funeral home offers direct cremation, it must make alternative containers available to consumers. The funeral home must also list the range of its highest and lowest priced direct cremations on the GPL.

(16) **Immediate Burial**. An immediate burial is a disposition of the body by burial, without formal viewing, visitation or ceremony with the body present, except that it may contain a graveside service. The price listing for immediate burials is very similar to direct cremation. The funeral home must provide a range of the lowest and highest priced immediate burial package offerings. It is also required to present various immediate burial package options, including the price of an immediate burial if the purchaser supplies his or her own container.

c. *Mandatory Disclosures.*

There are six separate mandatory disclosures with must appear on the GPL. On the sample GPL that has been placed in the appendix to this chapter, the six mandatory disclosures appear in italicized print so that you can identify them.

Funeral directors are prohibited from editing or modifying the mandatory disclosures. They should appear on the funeral home's General Price List in the exact wording which is provided in the sample model. Also, the mandatory disclosures must be printed in a clear and conspicuous manner. This means that the mandatory disclosure should not appear in smaller type than the other printed materials on the GPL.

The six mandatory disclosures are as follows:

(1) **Choice of Goods and Services**. The first mandatory disclosure on the GPL sample is the disclosure that informs consumers of their right to choose any goods and services they wish. This disclosure should be printed immediately above the itemized price listings of the sixteen goods and services described above.

(2) **Non-Declinable Service Fee**. Under the Basic Services of Funeral Director and Staff on the sample GPL, the second mandatory disclosure is printed. This mandatory disclosure informs consumers that the basic service fee is non-declinable and that it has been included in the charges for direct cremation, immediate burial, and forwarding and receiving of remains. This mandatory disclosure must be made in immediate conjunction with the listing of the Basic Services of Funeral Director and Staff.

(3) **Embalming Disclosure**. In conjunction with the embalming listing, consumers must be informed of their right to decline embalming. The mandatory disclosure which accompanies the embalming price listing on the GPL sample is designed to accomplish this purpose. This disclosure must be printed in immediate conjunction with the price listing for embalming.

(4) **Availability of Casket Price Lists**. On page 2 of the sample GPL the funeral home has listed its casket price range. Immediately under the casket price range a mandatory disclosure informs consumers about the availability of a complete price list at the funeral home.

(5) **Availability of Outer Burial Container Price Lists**. As with the casket price range, in immediate conjunction with the outer burial container price range, the funeral home must print the mandatory disclosure which informs consumers that a complete price list of outer burial containers will be provided at the funeral home.

(6) **Alternative Containers for Direct Cremation**. At the bottom of page 2 of the sample GPL there is a listing for direct cremations. Under that listing appears the mandatory disclosure that informs consumers that they may use an alternative container. The disclosure also briefly describes the alternative container sold by the funeral home. This disclosure must be made in immediate conjunction with the direct cremation listing.

d. *Package Funerals.*

Although funeral homes are required to itemize funeral goods and services, they are free to offer package selections. In other words, the funeral home can assemble different packages of goods and services and assign one price to them. Additionally, if the funeral home wishes, it may offer these packages at a discount as compared to its itemized pricing. For example, where a traditional funeral selected from the listing of itemized goods and services may cost $4,000, the funeral home could package those goods and services comprising a traditional funeral service and offer it for a package price of $3,500.

While the funeral home is free to offer package pricing, it is important to remember that it must be offered in addition, and not in lieu of, itemized pricing.

e. Distribution of GPL.

The GPL must be given for retention to individuals who inquire in person regarding funeral services, specific funeral goods or services, or the prices offered by the funeral home. Whenever there is any face-to-face discussion concerning the overall type of funeral service or disposition, specific funeral goods or funeral services, or the prices for those items, a GPL must be physically handed to the individual making the inquiry. It is not sufficient for the funeral director to simply indicate that a GPL is available if one is wanted.

The GPL distribution requirement is triggered wherever the face-to-face inquiry is made. Therefore, if a funeral director is removing a body from a residence, nursing home or hospital and the family inquires about funeral arrangements, a GPL must be distributed to them. Similarly, since the Funeral Rule applies to preneed arrangements as well as at-need arrangements, the distribution of the GPL should be made to all preneed consumers.

The GPL is to be given to individuals for their retention. Therefore, it is a violation of the Rule to charge a consumer for a copy of the GPL or to require the consumer to return the GPL to the funeral director. It is also improper to place the GPL in a binder or notebook which would implicitly suggest to the consumer that the GPL is not to be retained.

14.3 Casket Price List

If the GPL does not list the retail prices of the caskets offered by the funeral home, a separate Casket Price List must be prepared. This price list is far less complicated than the GPL. Although there are certain items which must appear on the list, there are no mandatory disclosures required on the casket price list.

a. Introductory Matters.

On the Casket Price List, the funeral home must place the name of the funeral home, the words "Casket Price List", and the effective date of the Casket Price List.

b. Casket and Alternative Container Listings.

All caskets and alternative containers which a funeral home has in stock for sale or which are part of the funeral home's regular offerings must be listed on the Casket Price List, together with the retail price of each. Caskets which require special ordering need not appear on the price list. There are no requirements regarding what order the caskets and containers must be listed nor are there any requirements concerning what type of caskets must be stocked. However, if the funeral home offers direct cremation, it is required to make an alternative container or an unfinished wood box readily available.

In listing the caskets and alternative containers, the funeral home should provide a brief description of the exterior construction and the interior lining. With metal caskets, the funeral home should list the gauge of the metal. If there is prominent exterior trimming or coloring, this should be noted on the Casket Price List. There is no requirement that the manufacturers, model names, or model numbers be identified.

c. Distribution of Casket Price List.

The Casket Price List must be presented to consumers upon the commencement of a face-to-face discussion about offerings on the Casket Price List or the price of those offerings. The Funeral Rule makes clear that the list should, at a minimum, be distributed to the consumer prior to the funeral director showing casket models to the consumer.

Unlike the General Price List, the Casket Price List does not have to be offered to consumers for their retention. A funeral director may request that the list be returned after the caskets have been shown.

The Funeral Rule allows the Casket Price List to be prepared in alternative formats such as binders, notebooks, brochures and charts.

14.4 Outer Burial Container Price List

The requirements of the Outer Burial Container Price List are very similar to the Casket Price List. They are as follows:

a. Introductory Matters.

The name of the funeral home, the words "Outer Burial Container Price List" and the effective date of the Outer Burial Container Price List must be printed at the top of the price list.

b. Outer Burial Container Listings.

All containers which the funeral home regularly offers should be listed on the Outer Burial Container Price List. Containers that need to be specially ordered are not required to appear on the list. If a funeral home does not offer outer burial containers to its customers, there is no requirement that it prepare an Outer Burial Container Price List.

A brief description of the exterior of the outer burial container should be provided on the price list. Manufacturers, model names, and model numbers need not be listed. In addition, the containers may be listed in any particular order which the funeral home prefers.

c. Mandatory Disclosure.

As can be seen from the italicized language on the sample Outer Burial Container Price List which appears in the appendix, there is a mandatory disclosure which must appear on the Outer Burial Container Price List. That disclosure informs consumers that outer burial containers are not generally required by law, although many cemeteries make them mandatory. That disclosure may be printed anywhere on the Outer Burial Container Price List.

d. Distribution of Outer Burial Container Price List.

Whenever there is a discussion of outer burial containers, the funeral director should present to the consumer the Outer Burial Container Price List. As with the Casket Price List, the Outer Burial Container Price List should be given to consumers prior to the funeral director showing any displays or models. The Outer Burial Container Price List need not be given for retention. In addition, the funeral home may utilize brochures, notebooks and charts in lieu of a printed Outer Burial Container Price List.

14.5 Statement of Funeral Goods and Services Selected

a. Itemized Listings.

The purpose of the Statement of Funeral Goods and Services Selected ("Statement") is to provide consumers with an itemized list of their purchases at the conclusion of the funeral arrangement. To accomplish this, the listings on the Statement must reflect the listings on the GPL. In other words, all separate goods and services which the consumer purchases off the GPL must be identified and listed on the Statement. The itemized price of each good and service must also be written on the Statement. It is improper to lump together on the Statement goods and services which are separately itemized on the GPL. For example, it would be improper to group together all of the separate automotive charges under one fee.

If a consumer purchases a package funeral, the funeral director should list the purchase of the package on the Statement together with the package price. In addition, the funeral director should list on the Statement each good and service that is included in that package. While it is not necessary for the funeral director to separately list the price of each good and service in the package, it is necessary that the consumer have a listing of each good and service that comprises the package.

In addition to the goods and services purchased from the funeral home, the Statement should also list any cash advance items which the consumer purchased through the funeral home. If the actual price of the cash advance item is not known, the funeral director should make a reasonable estimate of the price of the cash advance item on the Statement.

b. Mandatory Disclosures.

There are two and possibly three mandatory disclosures which funeral homes must make on the Statement of Funeral Goods and Services Selected. Those disclosures are as follows:

(1) **Listing of Legal and Other Requirements**. At the top of the sample Statement in the appendix is the mandatory disclosure which informs consumers that they will only be charged for those items that they selected or that are required. This mandatory disclosure may be printed anywhere on the Statement, although most funeral homes prefer to put it at the top of the Statement.

The companion requirement to this disclosure is the provision of the Rule which mandates that a funeral home lists on the Statement any legal, cemetery or crematory requirements which compel the consumer to purchase a specific good or service. For example, if state law requires embalming or if the cemetery has a regulation which dictates that outer burial containers must be utilized, those requirements should be listed by the funeral director on the Statement. On the second page of the sample Statement in the appendix, there is a space on the Statement for the funeral director to list laws or regulations which compel the purchase of a good or service.

(2) **Embalming Approval**. The second paragraph at the top of the Statement contains the mandatory disclosure which explains to consumers the requirements for embalming. As with the previous disclosure concerning legal and cemetery requirements, this disclosure may appear anywhere on the Statement. This disclosure also has a companion requirement which mandates that the funeral director list on the Statement the reason why embalming was performed. On the second page of the sample Statement in the appendix, a blank line has been provided for the funeral director to list the reason why the embalming was selected. Typical reasons include family consent, interstate transportation of remains, or public visitation.

(3) **Marked-Up Cash Advances**. If a funeral home adds a surcharge to a cash advance item or if it receive and retains a rebate, commission or other discount from the supplier of that cash advance item that is not passed

on to the consumer, the funeral home has marked-up the cash advance. The Funeral Rule requires funeral homes to identify on the Statement those particular cash advance items that have been marked-up. At the bottom of the cash advance listings on the first page of the sample Statement the required mandatory disclosure appears under which the funeral director would identify those cash advance items that have been marked-up.

If the funeral home never marks-up a cash advance item, it does not have to print this disclosure on the Statement. It should also be noted that the funeral home does not have to identify the dollar amount of the mark-up. It merely has to indicate those cash advance items that have been marked-up. This disclosure must be made in immediate conjunction with the listing of the cash advance items.

c. *Distribution of Statement.*

The presentation of the Statement is to be made at the conclusion of the funeral arrangements. It should be completely filled out and show the total price of the funeral. Signatures are not required on the Statement, although it is recommended since the Statement can serve as the funeral contract. If arrangements are made pursuant to a telephone call, the Statement should be promptly mailed to the consumer.

14.6 Telephone Price Disclosures

Whenever an individual telephones a funeral home and asks about the funeral home's offerings or prices, the funeral home must provide accurate information in response to those inquiries. The funeral home is prohibited by the Funeral Rule from refusing to give price information over the telephone. Moreover, the funeral director cannot insist upon the caller identifying himself or herself as a condition to the disclosure of price information over the telephone.

If a funeral director or trained staff member is not available to provide the requested information, a message should be taken and the call should be promptly returned by the funeral director. Similarly, messages taken by answering machines or answering services must be promptly returned.

14.7 Misrepresentations

The Funeral Rule prohibits misrepresentations in the six specific areas listed below. In addition, the Funeral Rule has prescribed several mandatory disclosures (all of which were discussed earlier) which the FTC believes are necessary to prevent consumers from being misled in these areas.

a. *Embalming.*

The Rule prohibits any misrepresentations regarding the legal necessity of embalming. It is furthermore a violation of the Rule if the funeral director fails to inform the consumer that embalming is not required by law, except in special circumstances. By placing the mandatory disclosure regarding embalming on the GPL, the funeral director has complied with his obligation to inform the consumer regarding embalming.

It is also a violation of the Funeral Rule to inform consumers that embalming is required as a practical necessity in the following cases:

(1) When the consumer wishes to have a direct cremation;

(2) When the consumer wishes to have an immediate burial; or

(3) If refrigeration is available **and** there is to be a funeral with no viewing **and** there is to be a closed casket.

b. Caskets for Direct Cremation.

The Rule prohibits a funeral director from representing that state or local law requires a casket for direct cremation. In addition, if a funeral home offers direct cremation, it must have alternative containers available for direct cremation consumers.

c. Outer Burial Containers.

It is a violation of the Funeral Rule to misrepresent that outer burial containers are required by law when such is not the case. It is also a violation of the Rule for the funeral home to fail to affirmatively inform consumers that state law does not require outer burial containers. This duty to affirmatively inform consumers is satisfied by the printing of the required mandatory disclosure on the Outer Burial Container Price List.

Misrepresentations regarding cemetery rules and regulations on outer burial containers are also prohibited by the Funeral Rule. As a precaution against such misrepresentations, funeral directors should obtain updated rules and regulations of local cemeteries so that they are knowledgeable concerning outer burial container requirements.

d. Legal and Cemetery Requirements.

The Funeral Rule provides a catchall prohibition against any type of misrepresentation concerning legal or cemetery requirements. In addition, funeral directors are required to list and describe on the Statement of Funeral Goods and Service Selected any legal, cemetery or crematory requirements that compel the consumer to purchase the funeral good or service.

e. Preservative and Protective Claims.

Funeral directors may not represent to consumers that funeral goods or services will delay natural decomposition or remains for a long or indefinite period. While the Rule does not prohibit funeral directors from explaining that embalming provides a temporary preservation to the body, it does prohibit any claims that embalming (or any other goods or services) will preserve the body for a long or indefinite period of time.

Funeral directors are also prohibited by the Funeral Rule from making misrepresentations regarding the protective features of caskets and vaults. Any claim regarding the ability of caskets and vaults to protect the body from graveside substances should not be made unless they can be substantiated.

f. Cash Advance Items.

If a funeral director marks up cash advance items or receives a commission, rebate or discount which is not passed on to the consumer, it is a violation of the Funeral Rule to represent to the consumer that the charge represents the same amount that the funeral home paid for these items. It is furthermore a violation if the consumer is not informed which particular cash advance items have been marked up. As seen earlier, the funeral director is to identify on the Statement those cash advance items that have been marked up.

14.8 Tying Arrangements

A tying arrangement exists where a seller requires a purchase of an unwanted item in order to obtain a desired good or service. For example, if a funeral director only offers funeral services if the consumer agrees to purchase a casket from the funeral home, the seller has tied the provision of funeral services to the required purchase of a casket. This violates the Funeral Rule.

The Funeral Rule prohibits tying arrangements except in the following three circumstances:

a. Non-Declinable Basic Service Fee.

As discussed earlier, the fee for the Basic Services of Funeral Director and Staff may be non-declinable by the funeral director. In other words, it is not a violation of the Rule to require consumers to pay this charge as a condition of receiving funeral services. All other fees, however, must be declinable unless one of the exceptions listed below applies.

b. Legal Requirements.

To the extent that state or local law requires the purchase of a funeral good or service, the funeral director may tie the purchase of that good or service to the provision of funeral services. For example, if state law requires embalming of contagious disease cases, the funeral director may require embalming of all contagious disease cases as a condition of providing funeral services.

   c. *Impossible, Impractical or Excessively Burdensome.*

The Funeral Rule provides that funeral directors are not required to honor a request for a combination of goods and services that would be "impossible, impractical or excessively burdensome" to provide. Although the funeral director will have to make the initial judgment as to what is "impossible, impractical or excessively burdensome," the ultimate judgment would be made by the FTC if a Rule violation is charged.

The practical necessity of embalming is one area which falls under this exception. For example, a funeral director may refuse a family's request for the pubic viewing of an unembalmed body on the grounds of practical necessity. It may be offensive to members of the public to view an unembalmed body. Embalming in such circumstances is widely recognized as a practical necessity. On the other hand, if the family requests a brief viewing of an unembalmed body just for family members, the funeral director cannot refuse this request.

14.9 Prior Permission to Embalm

It is a violation of the Funeral Rule to charge for embalming except in the following circumstances:

   a. *State or Local Law.*

Whenever state or local law requires embalming, it is not a violation of the Funeral Rule to charge for embalming that was not authorized by the family. However, funeral directors would be required to note on the Statement that embalming was performed because of a legal requirement.

   b. *Prior Permission to Embalm.*

A charge for embalming may be made when the family provides express permission to embalm prior to embalming. It is important to note that the permission to embalm must be expressly provided; it cannot be implied. For example, this requirement is not met if the family gives the funeral director permission to "prepare the body" or if the family desires a funeral service that requires embalming. The funeral director must specifically ask the family for permission to embalm and must receive the permission prior to embalming.

If a funeral director embalms the body prior to receiving permission and if none of the other two exceptions (legal requirements or exigent circumstances) exist, the funeral director may not charge for embalming. This is true even if the family later provides the funeral director with permission to embalm. Charging for embalming under these circumstance constitutes a violation of the Rule.

  c. Exigent Circumstances.

  In order to fall under the exigent circumstances exception, all three of the following conditions must be fulfilled:

  (1) The funeral director is unable to contact a family member or other authorized person after exercising due diligence; and

  (2) The funeral director has no reason to believe that the family does not want embalming; and

  (3) After embalming the body, the funeral director informs the family that if they choose a funeral that does not require embalming, no embalming fee will be charged, but that a fee will be charged if they select a funeral that does require embalming. If the family then selects a funeral requiring embalming, the funeral director may charge for embalming.

14.10 Retention of Price Documents

  Funeral directors are required by the Funeral Rule to retain all price lists for a one year period from the date the price lists were last distributed. Therefore, if a funeral home updates its price list on January 1, 1995, it should retain the prior list until January 1, 1996.

  A copy of the Statement of Funeral Goods and Services Selected should be retained for a one year period from the date of the arrangement conference. After the one year time period has elapsed, the funeral director is allowed under the Funeral Rule to dispose of outdated price lists and old statements. Funeral directors should note, however, that certain states may require a longer period of document retention then the Funeral Rule.

14.11 Enforcement

  The Funeral Rule is enforced by the Federal Trade Commission. The FTC Staff will respond to complaints from consumers or others regarding violation of the Funeral Rule. In the past, fines in the range of $10,000 to $100,000 have been assessed against funeral homes for violations of the Rule. In some cases, the funeral homes have been required to refund money back to certain consumers.

APPENDIX

GENERAL PRICE LIST

Effective Date: _____

The goods and services shown below are those we can provide to our customers. You may choose only the items you desire. However, any funeral arrangements you select will include a charge for our basic services. If legal or other requirements mean you must buy any items you did not specifically ask for, we will explain the reason in writing on the statement we provide describing the funeral goods and services you selected.

Basic Services of Funeral Director and Staff .... $ _____

Our fee for the basic services of funeral director and staff include conducting the arrangement conference, planning the funeral, shelter of remains, obtaining necessary permits, and placing obituary notices. *This fee for our basic services will be added to the total cost of the funeral arrangements you select. (This fee is already included in our charges for direct cremations, immediate burials, and forwarding or receiving remains.)*

Embalming .... $ _____

Except in special certain cases, embalming is not required by law. Embalming may be necessary, however, if you select certain funeral arrangements, such as a funeral with viewing. If you do not want embalming, you usually have the right to choose an arrangement that does not require you to pay for it, such as direct cremation or immediate burial.

Other Preparation of the Body

    A. Washing and disinfecting unembalmed remains .... $ _____

    B. Hairdresser .... $ _____

    C. Casketting and Dressing .... $ _____

Additional Services and Facilities

    A. Visitation .... $ _____

    B. Funeral Ceremony .... $ _____

    C. Memorial Service .... $ _____

    D. Graveside Funeral Service .... $ _____

Automotive Equipment

    A. Transfer of Remains to Funeral Home .... $ _____

    B. Hearse .... $ _____

    C. Limousine .... $ _____

Caskets .... $ _____ to $ _____

A complete price list will be provided at the funeral home.

Outer Burial Containers .... $ _____ to $ _____

A complete price list will be provided at the funeral home.

Forwarding Remains to Another Funeral Home .... $ _____

This charge includes removal of remains, basic services of staff, embalming, necessary authorizations and local transportation to airport. This charge does not include any rites or ceremonies.

Receiving the Remains from Another Funeral Home .... $ _____

This charge includes basic services of staff, pick up of remains, and transportation of remains to the cemetery. This charge does not include any rites or ceremonies.

Immediate Burials .... $ _____ to $ _____

This charge includes removal of remains, local transportation to the cemetery, and basic services of the staff. This charge does not include any rites or ceremonies.

    A. Immediate burial with casket
       provided by purchaser .... $ _____

    B. Immediate burial with casket
       selected from our funeral home
       (in addition to cost of casket) .... $ _____

Direct Cremations .... $ _____ to $ _____

This charge includes removal of remains, local transportation to crematory, and basic services of staff. This charge does not include any rites or ceremonies. *If you want to arrange a direct cremation, you can use an alternative container. Alternative containers encase the body and can be made of materials like fiberboard or composition materials (with or without an outside covering). The containers we provide are (specify containers).*

    A. Direct cremation with container provided by purchaser ... $ _____

    B. Direct cremation with alternative container .... $ _____

_____FUNERAL HOME

CASKET PRICE LIST

These prices are effective as of _____, but are subject to change without notice.

1. 20 ga. Steel, Protective Type, Velvet Interior .... $ _____
2. 18 ga. Steel, Bronze Tone, Protective Type, Crepe Int. . $ _____
3. Solid Bronze, Plated, Protective Type, Velvet Interior .... $ _____
4. Solid Copper, Protective Type, Crepe Interior .... $ _____
5. Solid Bronze, Scratch finish, Protective Type, Velvet Int. $ _____
6. 20 ga. Steel, Non-Protective Type, Twill Interior .... $ _____
7. 20 ga. Steel, Light Grey, Protective Type, Twill Interior .. $ _____
8. Solid Poplar, Velvet Interior ....$ _____
9. Solid Maple, Crepe Interior ....$ _____
10. Solid Oak, Velvet Interior ....$ _____
11. Solid Cherry Wood, Velvet Interior .... $ _____
12. Solid Pine, Crepe Interior ....$ _____
13. Soft Wood, Cloth Covered, Twill Interior .... $ _____
14. Heavy Cardboard, Wood Bottom (Cremation) .... $ _____

DISCLAIMER OF WARRANTIES

THE FUNERAL HOME MAKES NO REPRESENTATIONS OR WARRANTIES REGARDING THE CASKETS LISTED ABOVE. THE ONLY WARRANTIES, EXPRESSED OR IMPLIED, GRANTED IN CONNECTION WITH CASKETS SOLD ARE THE EXPRESS WRITTEN WARRANTIES, IF ANY, EXTENDED BY THE MANUFACTURERS THEREOF. THE FUNERAL HOME HEREBY EXPRESSLY DISCLAIMS ALL WARRANTIES, EXPRESSED OR IMPLIED, RELATING TO THE CASKETS, INCLUDING, BUT NOT LIMITED TO THE IMPLIED WARRANTIES OF MERCHANTABILITY AND FITNESS FOR A PARTICULAR PURPOSE.

_____FUNERAL HOME

OUTER BURIAL CONTAINER PRICE LIST

These prices are effective as of _____, but are subject to change without notice.

In most areas of the country, state or local law does not require that you buy a container to surround the casket in the grave. However, many cemeteries require that you have such a container so that the grave will not sink in. Either a grave liner or a burial vault will satisfy these requirements.

Concrete Box .... $ _____

Concrete with Asphalt Finish .... $ _____

Concrete Strentex Liner .... $ _____

Concrete Marbelon Liner .... $ _____

Concrete Stainless Steel Liner

over Strentex Liner .... $ _____

Stainless Steel .... $ _____

DISCLAIMER OF WARRANTIES

THE FUNERAL HOME MAKES NO REPRESENTATIONS OR WARRANTIES REGARDING THE OUTER BURIAL CONTAINERS LISTED ABOVE. THE ONLY WARRANTIES, EXPRESSED OR IMPLIED, GRANTED IN CONNECTION WITH THE OUTER BURIAL CONTAINERS ARE THE EXPRESS WRITTEN WARRANTIES, IF ANY EXTENDED BY THE MANUFACTURERS THEREOF. THE FUNERAL HOME HEREBY EXPRESSLY DISCLAIMS ALL WARRANTIES, EXPRESSED OR IMPLIED, RELATING TO THE OUTER BURIAL CONTAINERS, INCLUDING, BUT NOT LIMITED TO, THE IMPLIED WARRANTIES OF MERCHANTABILITY AND FITNESS FOR A PARTICULAR PURPOSE.

_____**FUNERAL HOME**

STATEMENT OF FUNERAL GOODS
AND SERVICES SELECTED

Charges are only for those items that you selected or that are required. If we are required by law or by a cemetery or crematory to use any items, we will explain the reasons in writing below.

If you selected a funeral that may require embalming, such as a funeral with viewing, you may have to pay for embalming. You do not have to pay for embalming you did not approve if you selected arrangements such as a direct cremation or immediate burial. If we charged for embalming, we will explain why below.

_____

Funeral Services for

_____   _____
Date of Death   Date of Funeral Service

A.   PROFESSIONAL SERVICE SELECTED
Basic Services of Funeral
Director and Staff .... $ _____
Embalming .... $ _____
Other Preparation of the Body:
Casketing and Dressing .... $ _____
Disinfection of Unembalmed
Remains .... $ _____
Hairdresser .... $ _____

B.   ADDITIONAL SERVICES AND
FACILITIES FEES
Visitation .... $ _____
Funeral Service .... $ _____
Memorial Service .... $ _____
Graveside Funeral Service .... $ _____
Other:
.... $ _____
.... $ _____

C.   AUTOMOTIVE EQUIPMENT
(local service 25 miles)
Transfer of Remains to Funeral
Home .... $ _____
Funeral Coach .... $ _____
Limousine(s) .... $ _____
Other Automotive Equipment:
.... $ _____
.... $ _____

D.   ALTERNATIVE SERVICES
Forwarding Remains .... $ _____
Receiving Remains .... $ _____
Direct Cremation .... $ _____

Immediate Burial .... $ _____
TOTAL SERVICE SELECTED .... $ _____

E.   MERCHANDISE SELECTED
Casket .... $ _____
Outer Burial Container .... $ _____
Urn .... $ _____
Clothing .... $ _____
Registration Book .... $ _____
Acknowledgment Cards .... $ _____
Other: ....
Sales Tax .... $ _____
TOTAL MERCHANDISE SELECTED .... $ _____

****

F.   CASH ADVANCES
Cemetery Charges .... $ _____
Flowers .... $ _____
Clergy .... $ _____
Death Certificates .... $ _____
Other: .... $ _____
Clergy .... $ _____
Death Certificates .... $ _____
Other: .... $ _____

We charge you for our services in obtaining:
_____
_____

TOTAL CASH ADVANCES .... $ _____

TOTAL SERVICES, MERCHANDISE
AND CASH ADVANCES.. .... $ _____
Paid at or prior to arrangements,
or other credits .... $ _____

BALANCE DUE. .... $ _____

113

This is a cash transaction. The undersigned jointly and severally agree to pay _____ FUNERAL HOME the balance due on this account, plus the agreed value of such additional services, materials and cash advances as may be furnished by _____FUNERAL HOME. Such payment shall be made within thirty days from date of the funeral service. A late penalty of _____% per month (_____% per year) will be assessed on the unpaid balance for materials and services.

DISCLAIMER OF WARRANTIES

THE FUNERAL HOME MAKES NO WARRANTIES OR REPRESENTATIONS CON-CERNING THE PRODUCTS SOLD HEREIN. THE ONLY WARRANTIES, EXPRESSED OR IMPLIED, GRANTED IN CONNECTION WITH THE PRODUCTS SOLD WITH THIS FUNERAL SERVICE, ARE THE EXPRESSED WRITTEN WARRANTIES, IF ANY EXTENDED BY THE MANUFACTURERS THEREOF. THE FUNERAL HOME HEREBY EXPRESSLY DISCLAIMS ALL WARRANTIES, EXPRESS OR IMPLIED, RELATING TO ALL SUCH PRODUCTS, IN-CLUDING, BUT NOT LIMITED TO, THE IMPLIED WARRANTIES OF MERCHANTABILITY AND FITNESS FOR A PARTICULAR PURPOSE.

I/We, the undersigned, acknowledge that the foregoing statement has been read to me/us and I/we hereby acknowledge receipt of com-pleted copy.

If any law, cemetery, or crematory requirements have required the purchase of any of the items listed, the law or requirement is explained be-low:

_____   _____
(Purchaser)   (Purchaser)

_____

_____

_____   _____
(Address)   (Address)

Reason for Embalming:

_____

THE_____FUNERAL HOME

Date _____   _____
            Signature of funeral personnel

Chapter Fifteen

FEDERAL REGULATION OF FUNERAL
BILLING AND COLLECTION

15.1 Introduction

In addition to the Funeral Rule, funeral directors are also subject to a trio of federal consumer protection and disclosure measures that regulate billing and collection practices. Those provisions — the Truth-In-Lending Act and regulations, the Magnuson-Moss Warranty Act, and the Credit Practices Regulation — were enacted in the past two decades to remedy perceived abuses by retailers and creditors. Since funeral directors are retailers and sometimes act as creditors, it is vital that they possess a working knowledge of these provisions.

15.2 Truth-In-Lending

The purpose of the Federal Truth-In-Lending Act (15 USC §1601 et seq.) and the regulations issued pursuant to that Act (12 CFR §226 et seq.) is to insure that consumers who are provided credit by banks and businesses are fully apprised of all aspects of the credit arrangements. To this end, the Act requires a number of disclosures to be made by banks or businesses extending credit. Since some funeral directors do extend credit and since there is no exemption for funeral directors from the Truth-In-Lending disclosure requirements, it is important to understand under what circumstances funeral directors must make the Truth-In-Lending disclosures.

a. Coverage of the Act.

A funeral director will be required to make Truth-In-Lending disclosures during any particular transaction if he satisfies a two-part test: (1) he qualifies as a creditor under the regulations; AND (2) he extends credit to a consumer.

It is important to note that both of these conditions must be satisfied in order to make the Truth-In-Lending requirements applicable. Thus, if a funeral director extends consumer credit in a particular case, but he does not qualify as a creditor under the regulations, he need not make the required disclosures.

b. Definition of a Creditor.

As stated above, in order to be subject to the Act, a funeral director must be defined as a creditor. A creditor is defined under the regulations as a person or business which extends consumer credit more than 25 times in a year. In order for a funeral director to determine if he is a creditor under the Act, he must examine his transactions in the prior and present calendar year. For example, if a funeral director extended credit more than 25 times in 1995, he will be defined as a creditor for all of 1996. If he again extends consumer credit more than 25 times in 1996, he will be a creditor for 1997.

Likewise, if a funeral director extends credit 25 times or less during 1995, he will not be a creditor in 1996. However, as soon as he extends credit for the 26th time in 1996, he will be a creditor for the remainder of 1996 and all of 1997. The only way he will be able to lose his creditor status is to extend credit 25 times or less in 1997.

c. Definition of Consumer Credit.

A funeral director extends "consumer credit" whenever he imposes a finance charge in a transaction with a natural person OR he enters into a written agreement with a natural person that calls for payments by more than four installments.

Note that the arrangement must be with a natural person. If the obligor on the funeral bill is a company, the Truth-In-Lending requirements will not apply. This is also true if the obligor is the fiduciary such as a trustee, guardian, administrator or executor of an estate. Since the law does not regard these persons as "natural persons", a funeral director could extend them credit without being subject to the Truth-In-Lending requirements.

A few examples may clarify exactly when a funeral director will be required to make Truth-In-Lending disclosures.

(1) A funeral director has extended credit 30 times in 1995. In 1996 he orally agrees to allow a consumer to pay his bill in six installments without interest charges. Although the funeral director is defined as a "creditor" for all of 1996, he is not required to make a disclosure in this particular case because he is not extending credit. If the agreement were written or if interest charges were imposed, the disclosures would have to be made.

(2) A funeral director extends consumer credit only five times in 1995. By September, 1996, he has extended credit 25 times. On his next consumer transaction he agrees orally to allow a consumer to pay in three installments with a five percent finance charge. In this case the Truth-In-Lending disclosures must be made since the funeral director is extending credit (the finance charge) and he

116

is doing it for the 26th time in one year. He will now be defined as a creditor for the remainder of 1996 and all of 1997.

(3) A funeral director who has extended consumer credit 35 times in 1995 is called on January 2, 1996 by the decedent's sister who is serving as executrix of the estate. He orally agrees to allow the estate to pay the bill in installments with a finance charge. In this case the funeral director is a creditor for all of 1996 since he extended consumer credit more than 25 times in the previous year. He also would be regarded as extending consumer credit in this transaction, but for the fact that the obligor on the funeral bill is the estate of the decedent. Therefore, since he is not extending consumer credit to a natural person, the Truth-In-Lending disclosures are not applicable.

d. *Definition of a Finance Charge.*

As stated above, whenever a finance charge is imposed, a person is deemed to be extending credit. This raises the question as to what constitutes a finance charge. Two particular situations which concern funeral directors are the late charge and the discount for prompt payment.

Under the regulations, late charges imposed against consumers not making payments when due will not be considered to be finance charges. However, in order to distinguish a late charge from a normal finance charge, the funeral director must take certain precautions. His invoice or bill must state that the entire amount of the account is due by a certain date, and if not paid in full, a penalty or late charge will be imposed. He also must impose the charge against all violators on a consistent basis. Furthermore, if a bill is not paid by a certain date, he should warn the consumer by letter or phone call that the account is overdue and that penalties are being imposed. It is important that he establish some type of collection procedure and that he apply it against all consumers who fail to make payments when due.

In addition to the measures set out above, the funeral director must avoid referring to the late charge as an interest charge, finance charge, carrying charge, or service charge. It is important that his invoice clearly state that the charge is a late charge or penalty imposed for the failure to pay the entire amount of the bill when due.

With regard to discounts given to consumers who pay within a given time, it should be noted that, in many cases, these discounts constitute finance charges. For example, on a bill of $2,500.00, if a funeral director de-

117

ducts five percent for payment within 30 days, he is regarded as imposing a $125.00 finance charge. Thus, if a funeral director has the status of a creditor and gives discounts such as these, he must make all required Truth-In-Lending disclosures.

There are cases, however, in which discounts for prompt payment can be made without constituting an extension of credit. If a funeral director grants his customers the option to pay by credit card or to receive a discount for payment by cash or check, such a discount is not a finance charge. In order to qualify, however, this option must be made available to all customers. Furthermore, only discounts used in relationship with credit card transactions qualify for this special treatment.

e. Preneed Arrangements.

Those funeral directors who have entered into preneed arrangements must be cognizant of the fact that these arrangements may constitute extensions of consumer credit. If the funeral director imposes a finance charge, or if the customer pays for the funeral services in more than four installments pursuant to a written agreement, the preneed arrangements will be extensions of consumer credit. Therefore, funeral directors who enter into these particular types of preneed arrangements must be aware of the fact that if they are parties to 25 or more of these arrangements in one year, they will have the status of a creditor and will be required to make Truth-In-Lending disclosures.

f. Advertising.

Advertisements that list credit terms are governed by the Truth-In-Lending Act. The Act has two basic requirements with regard to advertisements. The first is that the specific credit terms listed in the advertisement, i.e., downpayment, amount that will be financed, annual percentage rate, must be the terms that actually are or will be arranged. Secondly, if the advertisement lists any of the following items: the amount of the downpayment required, the amount of any installment payment, the number of payments, the length of the repayment period or the amount of any finance charge, it must also list each of the following items: the amount of the downpayment, the terms of repayment, and the annual percentage rate, using that term. If the annual percentage rate is a variable rate, that fact must also be noted.

g. Refinancing and Extensions.

If a refinancing occurs, an entire set of new Truth-In-Lending disclosures must be made to the consumer. A refinancing takes place when the original credit obligation is replaced by a new credit obligation. If the original credit obligation is only extended or deferred, however, new Truth-In-Lending disclosures need not be made. Likewise, if the annual percentage rate is decreased, new Truth-In-Lending disclosures are not mandated. Finally, if the terms of the credit obligation are changed as a result of a court proceeding, e.g. bankruptcy, no new disclosures are required.

Even though an extension or deferral does not require the issuance of a new set of disclosures, various minor disclosures must be made if a fee is charged as a result of the extension or referral, and the credit obligation is not one in which the finance charge is determined simply by the application of a percentage rate to the unpaid balance. In that event, the creditor must set out the amount of the fee, the amount deferred or extended, and the date to which payment is deferred or extended.

    h.   *Required Disclosures.*

If a funeral director has the status of a creditor, he must make the disclosures listed below whenever he extends consumer credit. These disclosures must appear on a separate form from the funeral contract or bill and they must be made prior to the consummation of the sale.

    (1) **Amount Financed**. There are two disclosures required under this item. First, the consumer must be told the "amount financed" which is calculated by taking the cash price, adding any other amounts which are advanced by the funeral home but which are not part of the finance charge, and subtracting the downpayment and any prepaid finance charge. The funeral director, in making this disclosure, must use the term "amount financed" and must explain it as "the amount of credit provided to you or on your behalf."

    The second disclosure requires an itemized statement by the funeral director of the amount financed. The itemization, which is required to be listed separately from the rest of the disclosures, must state what amount was distributed directly to the consumer, what amount went to the payment of any prepaid finance charges, what amount was credited to the consumer's account with the funeral director, and what amounts were paid by the funeral director to other persons on the consumer's behalf. In regard to this last disclosure, a funeral director would be required to list all cash advance items, such as newspaper charges, cemetery charges, flower charges, etc. and the name of each person the funeral director paid.

119

However, in place of providing this itemization, the funeral director may provide a statement informing the consumer that he is entitled to a written itemization of the amount financed and a space for the consumer to indicate if he desires one. If the consumer does not elect to have one provided, the funeral director is excused from this requirement.

(2) **Finance Charge**. The funeral director must disclose that amount which he is charging to extend the credit. This must be referred to as the "finance charge" and it must be explained as "the dollar amount the credit will cost you." The finance charge is a total of all credit costs including interest, service charge, carrying charge, loan fee, finder fee or similar charges, time-price differential and credit reports. The cost of insurance premiums must be included as part of the finance charge, unless they are disclosed separately. The finance charge does not include taxes, license fees, legal fees, registration fees and the like.

Under the Truth-In-Lending regulations, if the amount financed is $1,000.00 or below and the finance charge stated is within $5.00 of the actual finance charge, the stated finance charge will be deemed accurate. For all amounts above $1,000.00, the regulations provide a tolerance of $10.00.

(3) **Annual Percentage Rate**. In making this disclosure. the funeral director must use the term "Annual Percentage Rate" and provide the explanation that this is "the cost of your credit as a yearly rate." If it is possible for this rate to be increased after the sale, the funeral director must disclose the circumstances under which the rate can be increased, how the increase would affect the consumer's payments, whether the increase has any limitations, and an example of the payment terms that would result from the increase.

Under the regulations, the stated annual percentage rate will be considered accurate if it is not more than one-eighth of one percent above or below the actual percentage rate. For irregular transactions, such as those where the payments are not equal, the tolerance is increased to one-fourth of one percent. In calculating the rate, creditors are permitted to disregard the fact that months have different numbers of days and the occurrence of leap year.

The easiest method to calculate the annual percentage rate is to obtain a copy of the Federal Reserve Board's Annual Percentage Rate Tables, Volume I. A copy may be obtained through the Federal Reserve System, Washington, D. C. 20551 or from any Federal Reserve Bank.

(4) **Payment Schedule**. The funeral director is required to disclose the payment schedule including the number, amount and timing of all payments. In the case of a demand obligation where there is no maturity date, the funeral director is required to disclose the due dates for interest payments for the first year only. In the event that the payments vary because the finance charges apply to an unpaid principal balance, the funeral director must disclose the largest and smallest payments in the series and explain that the payments may vary.

(5) **Total of Payments**. The funeral director must disclose the sum of payments under the payment schedule. He should do this under the heading "Total of Payments" and must explain that term as meaning "the amount you will have paid when you have made all scheduled payments."

(6) **Total Sale Price**. The total sale price is the sum of the cash price, the finance charge and any amount financed by the funeral director which was not included in the finance charge. The funeral director is required to use the term "Total Sale Price" in making this disclosure and must explain that it is "the total price of your purchase on credit, including your down payment of $_____."

(7) **Pre-Payment Penalty or Rebate**. The funeral director must state whether there is a penalty for prepaying the obligation. Likewise, if the funeral director provides a rebate for prepayment, he must so state.

(8) **Late Payment**. If a charge will be imposed against the consumer in the event of a late payment, the funeral director must disclose the amount of the penalty.

(9) **Security Interest.** If a security interest is obtained by the funeral director, he must disclose that fact and identify the secured property by type or item.

i.   Multiple Purchasers.

If two or more persons purchase the funeral, the Truth-In-Lending disclosures need be provided only to the primary obligor. If the two persons are joint and equal obligors, the disclosures may be given to either one of them. The funeral director should always provide the customer with the copy of the Truth-In-Lending disclosures and retain the original form for at least two years.

j.   Disclosure Examples.

A funeral costing $2,000.00 is paid for by a $500.00 downpayment and an agreement to pay off the remaining $1,500.00 in 12 equal installments at an interest rate of 15 percent. Assuming the funeral director was a "creditor", he would have to make the disclosures which are listed in Figure 15.A at the end of this Chapter.

A brief analysis will show how the disclosures listed in Figure 15.A were arrived at. The Amount Financed ($1,500.00) is the cash price of the funeral ($2,000.00) minus the downpayment ($500.00). The Finance Charge is $124.68. This was determined by adding up the amount of the payments that will be made ($1,624.68) and subtracting the Amount Financed ($1,500.00). If any additional fee such as credit reports or loan fees were charged to the borrower, these would have to be added on to the Finance Charge.

The Annual Percentage Rate is 15 percent. The Total of Payments ($1,624.68) is arrived at by simply adding up all the payments. The Total Sales Price ($2,124.68) is ascertained by adding the Total of Payments ($1,624.68) with the downpayment ($500.00). The Payment Schedule simply sets out the due dates of the payments. In this case, the amount of each payment was determined by using a comprehensive loan amortization book which is generally available at book stores. Finally, the amount of the late penalty is listed and the fact that no security interest has been taken is noted.

In the second example, a funeral director (who is a creditor) charges $2,000.00 for a funeral but provides for a four percent discount if payment is made within 20 days. Since he is a creditor and since the prompt payment discount qualifies as a finance charge, the disclosures listed in Figure 15.B would have to be made.

Looking at Figure 15.B, the first item is the Amount Financed. This is simply the cost of the funeral minus the discount. The next item, the Finance

122

Charge, is the amount of the cash discount. The Annual Percentage Rate is determined by a two-step process. First, divide the Finance Charge by the Amount Financed. Secondly, multiply that figure by a fraction which has 365 as its numerator (the number of days in a year) and as its denominator the number of days in which payment can be made and the discount received.

In order to clarify the above, we will go through the calculations we made on the sample form. The Amount Financed is $1,920.00, which is $2,000.00 (the cost) minus $80.00 (the discount). The Finance Charge is $80.00 (the discount). The Annual Percentage Rate was determined by dividing $80.00 by $1,920.00 which equals .0416 (4.16%). This figure was then multiplied by 365/20 which equaled the Annual Percentage Rate of 75.92%.

The next disclosure is the Total of Payments. This would simply be the cost of the funeral. The same applies to the Total Sale Price. This also would be the cost of the funeral. The Payment Schedule lists what amount the customer will pay if he makes payment by the discount date, and what amount he will pay if he makes payment after the discount date. Note that the only difference in Example Figure 15.A and this form occurs with this particular disclosure. Finally, the last two disclosures show what penalty the funeral establishment imposes for late charges and whether a security interest was taken.

15.3 Magnuson-Moss Warranty Act

The Magnuson-Moss Warranty Act (15 USC §2301 et seq.) is a federal statute which governs express and implied warranties. As a seller, funeral directors are providing warranties on the merchandise they sell even though they do not manufacture it. For example, when a funeral director sells a casket, he warrants by implication that the casket is structurally sound to hold the body. If the bottom falls out of the casket, the funeral director has breached those implied warranties.

a. Disclaimer of Warranties.

The law allows sellers of merchandise to disclaim these warranties, but only if the seller does it by using specific language that is presented to consumers in a clear and conspicuous manner. At the conclusion of this Chapter is Figure 15.C which is an example of an effective disclaimer of warranties. In order to disclaim warranties on the merchandise sold by funeral directors, it is advisable to place this disclosure in bold face print on Casket and Outer Burial Container Price Lists as well as the Statement of Funeral Goods and Services Selected.

b. Adoption of Manufacturers' Warranties.

Although the funeral director as a seller does not offer his own expressed warranties, many of the casket and vault manufacturers do offer warranties on their products. Funeral directors are generally not liable for warranties made by manufacturers. However, funeral director may be viewed as adopting those warranties if they make certain written or oral representations. For example, if a funeral director assures a consumer that a casket is water-tight, that funeral director may be viewed as the source of that warranty. Funeral directors should insure that they qualify all their claims by saying that it is the manufacturer which warrants that the casket is water-proof, etc. All representations regarding the casket should be tied to the manufacturers' warranties.

c. Display of Manufacturers' Warranties.

As a seller, funeral directors are obligated by law to make available to consumers copies of the manufacturers' warranties. The FTC has enacted regulations under the Magnuson-Moss Warranty Act which requires all sellers of consumer products to make available to prospective buyers, prior to sale, the text of any written manufacturer's warranty (16 CFR §700 et seq).

Funeral directors can comply with the FTC regulation in one of two ways. First, funeral directors can clearly and conspicuously display the text of the warranty in close conjunction with the product being sold. Secondly, funeral directors can maintain a binder or series of binders which contains each warranty. The binder should be labeled "WARRANTIES", should be properly indexed according to product, should be updated as new products are offered, and should be maintained in a location which provides the buyer with ready access to the binder. Either the binder or a sign advising the consumer of the binder's presence must be displayed in a manner reasonably calculated to draw the buyer's notice.

15.4 FTC Credit Practices Regulation

When a funeral director enters into a retail installment contract with a customer by which he permits the customer to pay for a funeral purchase over time through a note, account, or similar debt instrument, he must insure that the debt instrument is in compliance with the FTC's Credit Practices Regulation. There are six basic requirements with regard to consumer credit practices under the FTC's regulation. They are as follows:

a. Cognovit Note or Confession of Judgement.

It is a violation of the Federal Trade Commission Act for a funeral director, directly or indirectly, to take or receive from a consumer a debt instrument that constitutes or contains a cognovit or a confession of judgement, warrant of attorney, or other waiver of the right to notice and the opportunity to be heard in the event of suit or process thereon.

b. Executory Waiver.

Debt instruments utilized by funeral directors in retail installment sales to consumers may not constitute or contain an executory waiver or a limitation of exemption from attachment, execution, or other process on real or personal property held, owned by, or due to the consumer unless the waiver applies solely to property which is subject to the security interest which is executed in connection with the obligation. Since most goods sold by funeral directors cannot be attached in a collection suit, funeral directors' debt instruments should contain no executory waivers or limitation of exemptions from attachments.

c. Assignment of Wages.

The FTC Credit Practices Regulations also prohibits a debt instrument used by a retail installment seller in a consumer transaction from constituting or containing an assignment of wages or other earnings unless:

(1) the assignment by its terms is revokable at the will of the debtor, or

(2) the assignment is a payroll deduction plan or pre-authorized payment plan, commencing at the time of the transaction, in which the consumer authorizes a series of wage deductions as a method of making such payment, or

(3) the assignment applies only to wages or other earnings already earned at the time of the assignment.

d. Security Interest in Household Goods.

No debt instrument between a retail installment seller and a consumer may constitute or contain a non-possessory security interest in household goods other than a purchase money security interest. In other words, a funeral director may not take a security interest in clothing, furniture, applications, radios, televisions, linens, china, crockery, kitchenware, and personal effects (including wedding rings) of the consumer in order to secure the purchase of a funeral. It should be noted that works of art, electronic entertainment equipment (except one television and one radio), antiques (any item over 100 years old), and jewelry (except wedding rings) are not regarded as household goods, and therefore, may be used as security.

e. Co-signer Practices.

Under the Credit Practices Regulation, it is a deceptive act or practice for a lender or a retail installment seller to directly or indirectly misrepresent the nature or extent of a co-signer's liability. It is also a violation of the Act for a lender or a retail installment seller, directly or indirectly, to obligate a co-signer unless the co-signer is informed prior to being obligated, of the nature of the co-signer's liability. To prevent these deceptive acts, the following notice should be provided to all co-signers on a separate document:

"NOTICE TO CO-SIGNER"

You are being ask to guarantee this debt. Think carefully before you do. If the borrower doesn't pay the debt, you will have to. Be sure you can afford to pay if you have to, and that you want to accept this responsibility.

You may have to pay up to the full amount of the debt if the borrower does not pay. You may also have to pay late fees or collection costs, which increase this amount.

The creditor can collect this debt from you without first trying to collect from the borrower. The creditor can use the same collection methods against you that can be used against the borrower, such as suing you, garnishing your wages, etc. If this debt is ever in default, that fact may become part of your credit record.

This notice is not the contract that makes you liable for the debt."

f. Late Charges.

It is a violation of the Credit Practices Regulation for a lender or retail installment seller to levy a late charge on a payment which is otherwise a full payment for the applicable period when the only delinquency is attributable to late fees which were assessed on that installment. In other words, a late fee cannot be charged on a timely installment payment if the only problem with that payment is that it did not include a late charge payment for a previous delinquency.

APPENDIX

FIGURE 15.A
TRUTH IN LENDING
DISCLOSURE OF INFORMATION

Funeral Director's Name and Address

Buyer's Name and Address

AMOUNT FINANCED: $1,500.00.   The amount of credit provided to you or on your behalf. You have a right to receive at this time itemization of the Amount Financed.

_____ I want an itemization   _____ I do not want an itemization.

  Buyer's Initials   Buyer's Initials

FINANCE CHARGE: $124.68. The dollar amount the credit will cost you.

ANNUAL PERCENTAGE RATE: 15%. The cost of your credit as a yearly rate.

TOTAL OF PAYMENTS: $1,624.68. The amount you will have paid when you have made all scheduled payments.

TOTAL SALES PRICE: $2,124.68. The total price of your purchase on credit, including your downpayment of $ 500.00.

PAYMENT SCHEDULE:

Number of Payments	Amount of Payments	Due Date of Payments
12	$135.39	First of every month for 12 months

LATE PAYMENT: If the amount due is not fully paid by the due date, a penalty will be charged at the rate of 1.5% per month on the unpaid balance.

SECURITY INTEREST:

_____ You are giving a security interest in_____.

_____ You are not giving a security interest.

BUYER ACKNOWLEDGES RECEIPT OF A COMPLETED COPY OF THIS DISCLOSURE STATEMENT PRIOR TO CONSUMMATION OF THE CREDIT SALE . See Contract documents for any additional information about default and nonpayment.

_____   _____
        Date   Buyer's Signature

FIGURE 15.B
TRUTH-IN-LENDING
DISCLOSURE OF INFORMATION
CASH DISCOUNT TRANSACTION

Funeral Director's Name and Address
Buyer's Name and Address

AMOUNT FINANCED: $1,920.00. The amount of credit provided to you or on your behalf. You have a right to receive at this time an itemization of the Amount Financed.

_____ I want an itemization   _____ I do not want an itemization.
  Buyer's Initials   Buyer's Initials

FINANCE CHARGE: $80.00. The dollar amount the credit will cost you.

ANNUAL PERCENTAGE RATE: 75.92%. The cost of your credit as a yearly rate.

TOTAL OF PAYMENTS: $2,000.00. The amount you will have paid when you have made all scheduled payments.

TOTAL SALES PRICE: $2,000.00. The total price of your purchase on credit, including your downpayment of $ 0.00.

PAYMENT SCHEDULE:

You will pay 1 payment(s) of $1,920.00 if payment is made by 5/20/95, the termination date of the discount period.

You will pay 1 payment(s) of $2,000.00 if payment is not made until 5/31/95, the due date of the invoice.

LATE PAYMENT: If the amount due is not fully paid by the due date, a penalty will be charged at the rate of 1.5% per month on the unpaid balance.

SECURITY INTEREST:

_____ You are giving a security interest in_____.

_____ You are not giving a security interest.

BUYER ACKNOWLEDGES RECEIPT OF A COMPLETED COPY OF THIS DISCLOSURE STATEMENT PRIOR TO CONSUMMATION OF THE CREDIT SALE . See Contract documents for any additional information about default and nonpayment.

_____   _____
      Date   Buyer's Signature

FIGURE 15.C

DISCLAIMER OF WARRANTIES

_____FUNERAL HOME MAKES NO REPRESENTATIONS OR WARRANTIES REGARDING THE MERCHANDISE SOLD WITH THIS FUNERAL SERVICE. THE ONLY WARRANTIES, EXPRESSED OR IMPLIED, GRANTED IN CONNECTION WITH MERCHANDISE SOLD WITH THIS FUNERAL SERVICE ARE THE EXPRESS WRITTEN WARRANTIES, IF ANY, EXTENDED BY THE MANUFACTURERS THEREOF. NO OTHER WARRANTIES, EXPRESSED OR IMPLIED, INCLUDING THE IMPLIED WARRANTIES OF MERCHANTABILITY AND FITNESS FOR A PARTICULAR PURPOSE, ARE EXTENDED BY_____FUNERAL HOME.